The Hohokam Millennium

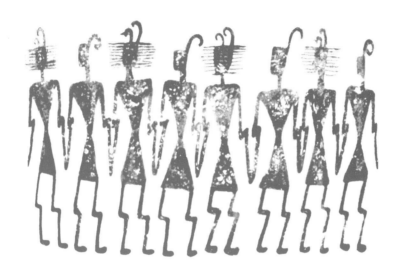

D1597256

The publication of this volume was made possible by generous gifts from
Maggie and Christian Andersson for the Loretto Chapel of Santa Fe and William S. Cowles,
and by grants from the Phoenix Area Office of the Bureau of Reclamation
and the Arizona Humanities Council.

Arizona
Humanities
Council

Sharing cultures. Enriching communities.

The Hohokam

A School for Advanced Research
Popular Southwestern Archaeology Book

Millennium

Edited by Suzanne K. Fish and Paul R. Fish

School for Advanced Research Press
Santa Fe, New Mexico

School for Advanced Research Press
Post Office Box 2188
Santa Fe, New Mexico 87504-2188
www.sarpress.sarweb.org

Co-Director and Executive Editor: Catherine Cocks
Copy Editor: Jane Kepp
Design and Production Manager: Cynthia Dyer
Maps: Molly O'Halloran
Proofreader: Kate Whelan
Indexer: Ina Gravitz
Printed by C&C Offset Printing in China

Library of Congress Cataloging-in-Publication Data
The Hohokam millennium / edited by Suzanne K. Fish and Paul R. Fish.
  p. cm. — (A School for Advanced Research popular southwestern archaeology book)
  Includes index.
  ISBN 978-1-930618-80-0 (cl : alk. paper) — ISBN 978-1-930618-81-7 (pa : alk. paper)
  1. Hohokam culture—Arizona—Phoenix. 2. Excavations (Archaeology)—Arizona—Phoenix.
    3. Phoenix (Ariz.)—Antiquities. I. Fish, Suzanne K. II. Fish, Paul R.
      III. School for Advanced Research (Santa Fe, N.M.)

E99.H68.H635 2007
979.101—dc22
2007024336

Cover photograph (front): Casa Grande Ruins National Monument © Adriel Heisey.
Cover photograph (back): Excavated room blocks at the Pueblo Grande Museum © Adriel Heisey.

Contents

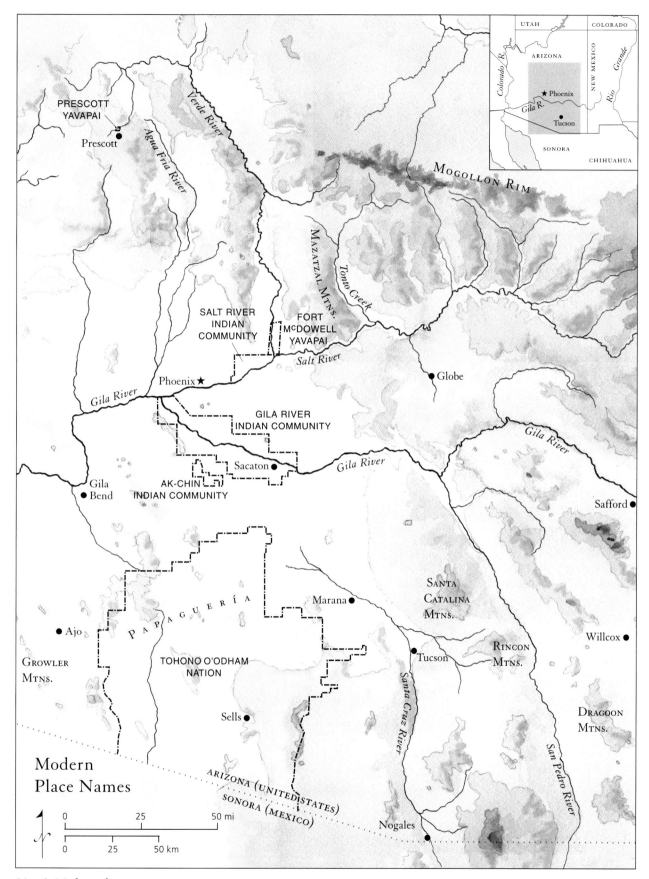

Modern
Place Names

Map 1. Modern place names.

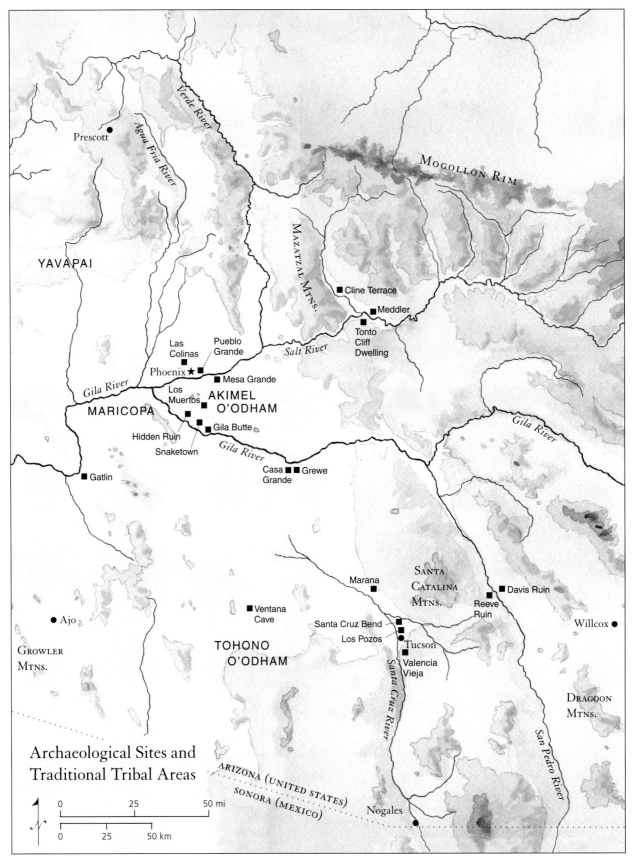

Map 2. Hohokam archaeological sites and traditional tribal areas after 1700 CE.

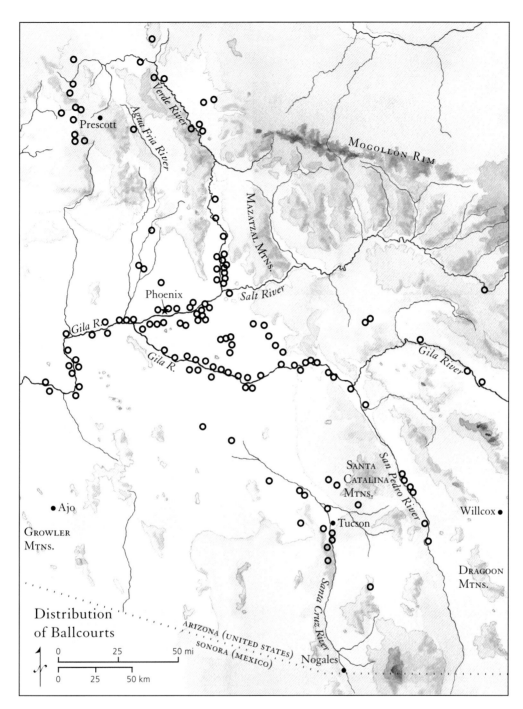

Map 3. Locations of Preclassic period Hohokam ball courts.

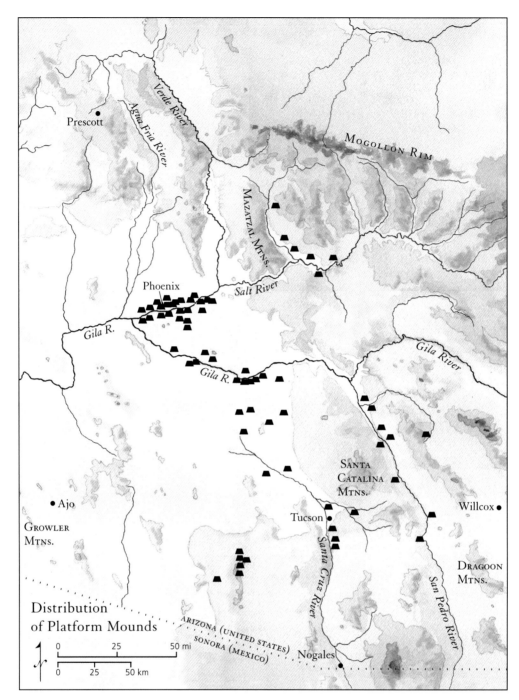

Map 4. Locations of Classic period platform mounds.

A Brief Chronology of the Hohokam Area

BCE (before the common era)

2000	Earliest corn in the Tucson Basin.
1600	Households store food in large pits.
1500	Earliest irrigation canals in the Tucson Basin.
1300	Early ceramic figurines and occasional tiny pots.
1200	Sustained occupation of floodplain by Tucson irrigators.

CE (of the common era)

200–450	Early Ceramic period: Everyday use of plain pottery; figurines used in household rituals.
450	The "Hohokam millennium" begins.
450–700	Pioneer period: Villages organized around central plazas; pithouse groups with shared courtyard; use of palettes and censers in rituals; large-scale irrigation in Phoenix Basin.
700–1150	Preclassic period (encompassing the Colonial and Sedentary periods).
700–900	Colonial period: Ball courts and red-on-buff pottery appear; Rillito Red-on-buff pottery trades widely.
900–1150	Sedentary period: Expanded irrigation in Phoenix Basin; widespread trade; early mounds used as dance platforms.
1150–1300	Early Classic period: Decline of ball court importance; regional reorganization; platform mounds become common public buildings.
1300–1450 or 1500	Late Classic period: Platform mounds expand; Puebloan migrants arrive; massive adobe architecture; population concentrates in fewer areas.
1450–1500	The Hohokam millennium ends; population abruptly declines.
1500–1700	Archaeological hiatus: Demographic collapse and disappearance of Hohokam culture; O'odham cultures develop in former Hohokam territory.
1700	Father Kino at Casa Grande ruins in 1694; San Xavier del Bac mission established.
1800	Akimel O'odham rebuild Hohokam canals on Gila River.
1900	Dams on Salt and Gila Rivers halt O'odham irrigation.
2000	Modern reservation system and tribal governments established.

For Emil Haury, first among Hohokam scholars.

The Hohokam Millennium

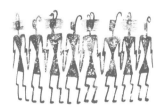

Figure 1.1. Thick-walled Hohokam censers made of pottery and stone during the Preclassic period resemble pre-Hispanic Mexican vessels used to burn aromatic substances as incense.

The Hohokam Millennium

Suzanne K. Fish and Paul R. Fish

Hot, dry regions of the world have produced some of the most memorable preindustrial civilizations, and the southern deserts of Arizona are no exception. The aptly named modern Phoenix, now the fifth largest city in the United States, arose not from the ashes but from the ruins of what was the most populous and agriculturally productive valley in the West before 1500 CE. When the early Southwestern archaeologist Frank Hamilton Cushing entered this Salt River valley in 1892, he climbed atop an earthen monument in what would become urban Phoenix and exclaimed at the discovery of "one of the most extensive ancient settlements we had yet seen.… Before us, toward the north, east, and south, a long series of…house mounds, lay stretched out in seemingly endless succession" (fig. 1.2). Entrepreneurs arriving from the eastern United States a few decades earlier had, like Cushing, seen not only house mounds but also the former courses of the most massive canals ever built in the pre-Columbian Americas north of Peru (fig. 1.2; plate 20). They soon reestablished large-scale irrigation by laying out new canals virtually in the footprints of the prehistoric ones, triggering the growth of the future city.

Figure 1.2. Centuries of weathering reduced Hohokam adobe buildings to low "house mounds" of earth. When excavated, the mounds often reveal well-preserved outlines of walls, as in this compound at Casa Grande National Monument excavated in 1908.

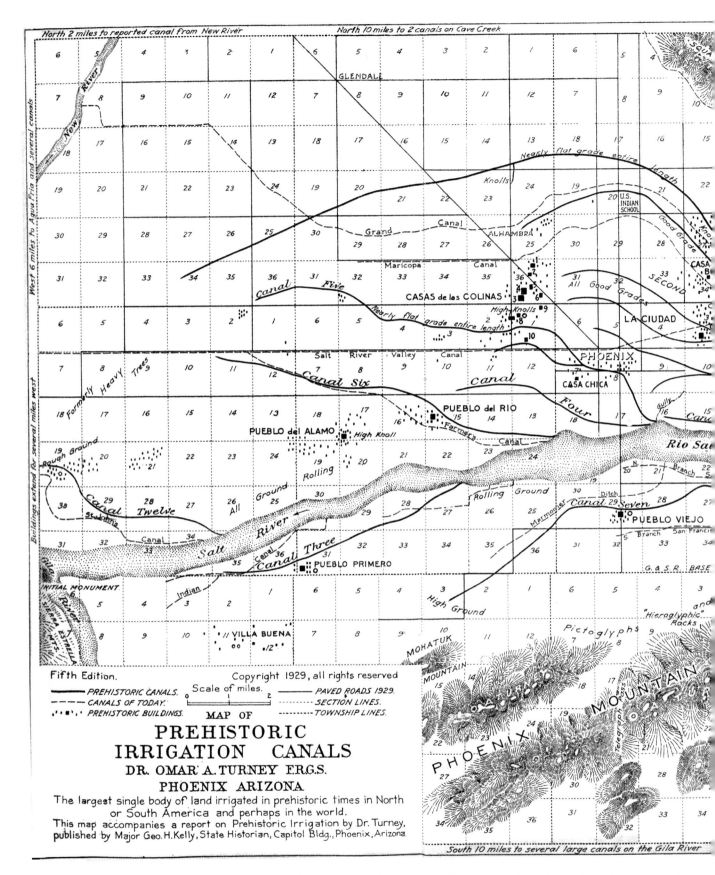

Figure 1.3. Omar Turney, engineer for the city of Phoenix, compiled this map of major Hohokam sites and canal systems in the

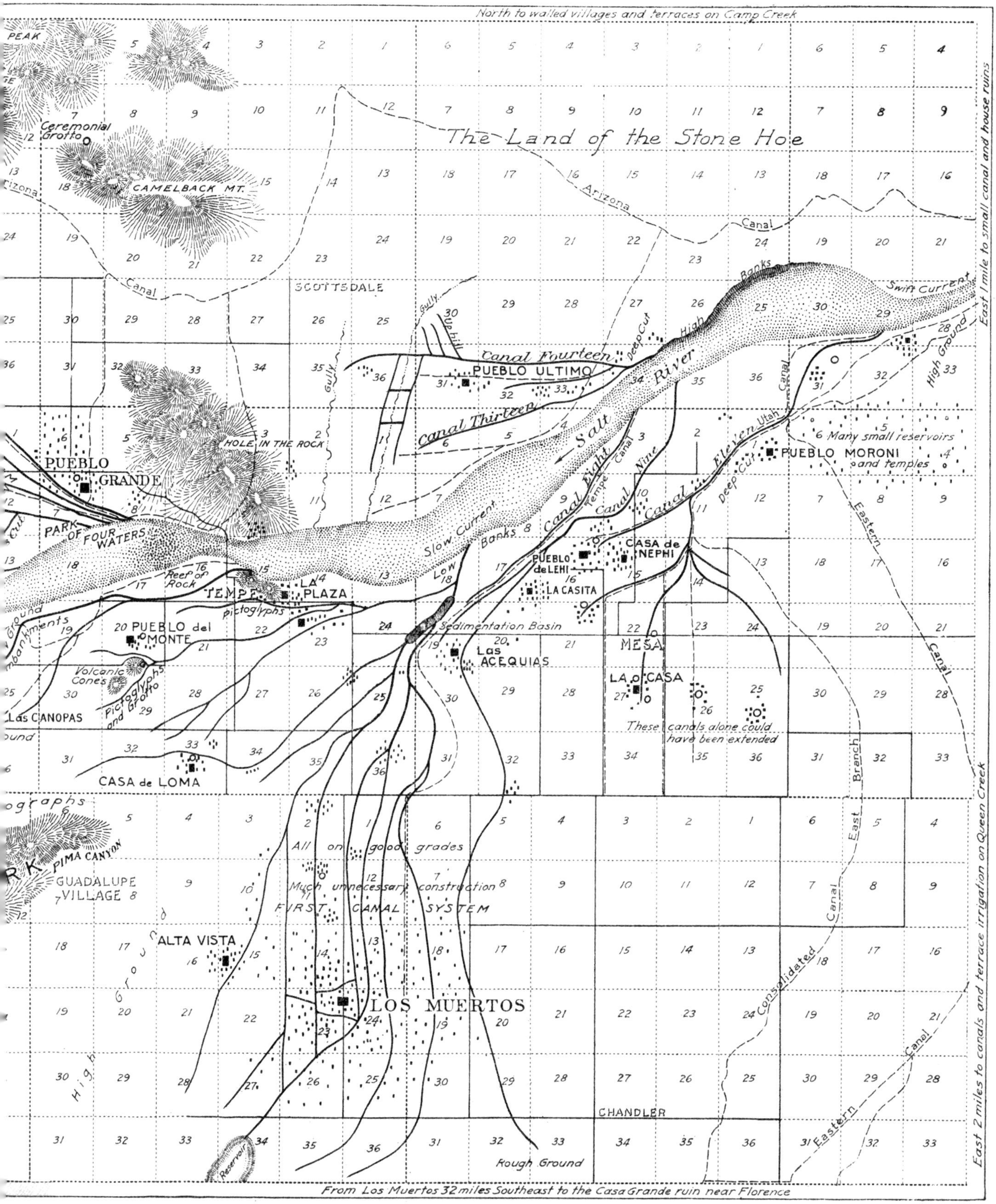
North to walled villages and terraces on Camp Creek
PEAK
Ceremonial Grotto
CAMELBACK MT.
The Land of the Stone Hoe
Arizona
Canal
SCOTTSDALE
Gully
Uphill
Canal Fourteen
Deep Cut
PUEBLO ULTIMO
Canal Thirteen
High Banks
Salt River
Swift Current
High Ground
Utah Canal
Canal Eleven
Deep Cut
Canal Nine
Tempe Canal
Canal Eight
PUEBLO MORONI
Many small reservoirs and temples
HOLE IN THE ROCK
PUEBLO GRANDE
PARK OF FOUR WATERS
Slow Current
Banks
Low
Reef of Rock
TEMPE
LA PLAZA
Pictographs
CASA de NEPHI
PUEBLO de LEHI
LA CASITA
Eastern Canal
Ground
Embankments
PUEBLO del MONTE
Sedimentation Basin
Las ACEQUIAS
MESA
LA CASA
Volcanic Cones
Pictographs and Grotto
Las CANOPAS
These canals alone could have been extended
CASA de LOMA
East Branch Canal
Pictographs
PIMA CANYON
GUADALUPE VILLAGE
All on good grades
Much unnecessary construction
FIRST CANAL SYSTEM
ALTA VISTA
High Ground
LOS MUERTOS
Consolidated Canal
Eastern Canal
CHANDLER
Reservoir
Rough Ground
From Los Muertos 32 miles Southeast to the Casa Grande ruin near Florence
East 1 mile to small canal and house ruins
East 2 miles to canals and terrace irrigation on Queen Creek

1920s, on the basis of earlier records and remains still visible at the time.

Figure 1.4. Partially excavated ball court at Snaketown. The earthen banks of ball courts enclosed the playing field and provided a vantage for spectators during ball games or other public events.

The remarkable people whom archaeologists call the Hohokam were the builders of the earthen monuments, adobe houses in profusion, and huge canals that so impressed later visitors to the Salt River Valley. From 450 to 1450 CE—the "Hohokam millennium"—the basin at the confluence of the Salt and Gila Rivers formed the core of their geographic and cultural domain. For 1,000 years the Hohokam maintained a recognizable cultural identity among the diverse peoples who inhabited other parts of the prehistoric Southwest and adjacent northwestern Mexico.

Who Were the Hohokam?
The fragments of buff to brown pottery with red painted designs (plate 5) that litter the low-lying basin floors of southern Arizona are the most distinctive and abundant material remains of former Hohokam residents. Ingenious farmers who employed an assortment of agricultural strategies to grow crops in arid terrain, they ultimately engineered irrigation networks surpassed in length and

size only by the canals of Andean empires. In addition to creating unique artifact styles, the Hohokam set themselves apart from the ancestral Pueblo, Mogollon, and other archaeological cultures of the Southwest by the forms of the public buildings in their largest villages. These ball courts (fig. 1.4) and platform mounds (plate 9) reflect the characteristic beliefs and community rituals of the Hohokam.

What might it have meant to individuals, household members, and villagers to have been participants in the Hohokam cultural sphere? It is difficult to answer this question from the fragments that have survived for archaeologists to examine. Yet the fact that they shared the same ways of making and decorating pottery, as well as other canons of style and utilitarian design, tells us that they were in close communication with one another and held common understandings about such matters. That they shared crops and farming technologies shows that they turned to the same solutions to meet the challenges of desert cropping. That they built the same sorts of structures for communal rituals implies that a shared set of beliefs guided them. But archaeologists cannot determine whether all the ancient Arizonans they classify as Hohokam spoke the same language, or whether they considered themselves to be members of the same ethnic group or culture.

Why these uncertainties over the meaning of being Hohokam? First, the distinctive archaeological remains that identify the Hohokam heartland are spread over an expanse of almost 30,000 square miles in the southern half of Arizona, an area larger than the state of South Carolina. The hallmarks of Hohokam culture are generally bounded by the upper reaches of the Agua Fria and Verde Rivers to the north, the Mogollon Rim to the northeast, the Dragoon Mountains to the southeast, the Mexican border to the south, and the Growler Mountains to the west (see map 1).

Within this far-flung territory, archaeological remains have much in common, but they also vary in important ways. Inhabitants of some sectors chose only parts of the overall cultural package to incorporate into their lives. For example, in the Tonto Basin, on the northeastern edges of the Hohokam domain, local people using red-on-buff pottery never built ball courts, although they eventually erected platform mounds. Migrations of Hohokam and non-Hohokam groups into the Tonto Basin contributed to the mixing of cultural practices. Where local groups shifted between full and incidental participation in Hohokam cultural traditions at different times, the archaeological boundaries for the Hohokam shift accordingly (see chapter 12).

A second reason for our uncertainties is the area's historic ethnic diversity. When Spanish explorers arrived in the late seventeenth century, they found Native Americans with diverse languages and life-styles all living in the former Hohokam domain. They included groups speaking primarily Piman languages (O'odham dialects) in the central portion, people speaking Yuman languages (Colorado River Yuman to the west and Yavapai to the north), and groups speaking Athabascan languages (Western Apache) in the northern and eastern reaches (see map 2). The diversity of the postcontact era suggests that the

Hohokam, too, might not have been homogeneous in all respects. It also complicates the question of how the prehistoric Hohokam are related to the succeeding native occupants of the same region (see chapter 15).

How Are the Hohokam Remarkable?

Among preindustrial societies throughout the world, the Hohokam hold the distinction of having constructed massive canal networks (up to 22 miles in length) and irrigated extensive tracts of land (up to 70,000 acres) in the absence of state-level government and a corresponding level of societal complexity. Archaeologists have not yet identified the graves or dwellings of rulers with such obvious high status and power that they could have imperiously resolved the inevitable disputes that arise among multitudes of water users or regulated the huge labor force needed to build and maintain the canals. Nor have archaeologists found evidence of a developed Hohokam bureaucracy that could have provisioned and organized workers. Yet the canal systems alone clearly required a tremendous amount of coordinated labor. Jerry Howard, an expert on Hohokam irrigation, estimates that it would have taken nearly a million person-days of labor to construct the trunk-lines of just one of the Phoenix Basin canal systems (see fig. 1.3). That figure does not include the additional effort needed to build secondary lines out to fields, clean out annual buildups of canal sediments, and make repairs after storms and floods.

The Hohokam also constructed earthen ball courts and platform mounds of modestly monumental size relative to those found elsewhere in the ancient world, again without all-powerful rulers or an established bureaucracy. The placement of these monuments imparted a unique pattern to Hohokam landscapes. Large villages with ball courts or platform mounds appear about every three miles along major canal lines in the Phoenix Basin and at greater intervals among surrounding settlements. The largest villages stood at the centers of clusters of smaller settlements, each cluster forming an organizational unit of population and territory that Hohokam archaeologists call a "community." The monuments in the centers served as

Figure 1.5. The Hohokam of the Preclassic period used carved stone palettes in household and public rituals.

staging areas for communal events unduplicated in outlying settlement zones. This characteristic mode of community organization both accommodated and shaped Hohokam economic, political, and ritual life (see chapter 5).

Ball courts and platform mounds are unusual in the US Southwest in their resemblance to the monumental forms of Mesoamerica, the heartland of the Toltec, Aztec, Maya, and other high cultures centered in what today is Mexico. Hohokam stylistic motifs and artifacts that are related to ritual and ideology, such as figurines, palettes, and censers, also show a pronounced Mesoamerican inspiration (figs. 1.1, 1.5). Many questions about the nature of this cultural connection linger unanswered because archaeologists until recently have mostly neglected the 400 miles of northwestern Mexico separating the Hohokam from the most likely west Mexican sources of such Mesoamerican traditions. (As chapter 7 shows, this situation is beginning to change.) A stronger Mexican connection than is seen elsewhere in the Southwest is further apparent in the

Hohokam trade for copper bells, iron pyrite mirrors, marine shells to make into jewelry, and a few other items that originated south of today's border.

The Hohokam are especially notable for the long-term continuity of their lifeways. In comparison with peoples in other parts of the Southwest, the Hohokam tended toward unusually prolonged residence in place. Once established, some clusters of dwellings in the largest settlements persisted—renovated, extended, and rebuilt—up to several hundred years. Central plazas in these foremost settlements remained the heart of village life from beginning to end. Successive generations lived in many of the largest settlements, amid irrigated land, for more than half the Hohokam millennium, and farming families returned again and again to outlying settlements where crops could be watered by alternative means. Settlement stability was an outcome of the productivity and sustainability of Hohokam agriculture. Sustainable production in turn was closely tied to places where enough water could be predictably captured and delivered to crops.

Figure 1.6. Saguaro, cholla, prickly pear, and small trees with edible beans supplied the Hohokam with important foods in the Sonoran Desert.

The Sonoran Desert Environment of the Hohokam

The great majority of Hohokam people lived within the outlines of the Sonoran Desert in southern Arizona and within the range of the towering saguaro cactus, one of its distinguishing species (fig. 1.6). Sonoran Desert vegetation differs from that of the Chihuahuan Desert to the east and the Mohave Desert to the west, thanks to rainfall that arrives in both winter and summer rather than mostly at one time of year. The two seasons of rainfall allow the Sonoran Desert to support large cacti such as saguaro and cholla and dryland trees such as mesquite, ironwood, and paloverde, in addition to the shrubs common to all three deserts. The fruits and buds of the cacti and the beanlike pods of the trees provided plentiful and reliable

wild staples in the Hohokam diet. Groves of mesquites and plants with edible small seeds, including saltbush, grasses, pigweed, and goosefoot, flourish along Sonoran Desert watercourses. For most of the meat they consumed, the Hohokam hunted jackrabbits, cottontails, and other small animals on land surrounding their homes and fields. As the human population increased, hunters had to go farther afield for large game, pursuing deer and bighorn sheep at higher elevations. The wild resources of the Sonoran Desert added variety, nutritional balance, and backup supplies in times of poor harvests.

Hohokam everywhere experienced the risks and opportunities of their Basin-and-Range environment. They focused their day-to-day lives as farmers on land in the basin interiors. They seldom

Figure 1.7. A street vendor in Guaymas, Sonora, sells sweet slices of baked agave hearts.

lived in the mountains at basin edges and only occasionally sought out upland resources. Temperatures typically topped 100° F on 90 days or more per year, and annual rainfall varied from 7 to 15 inches. The vast highland watersheds of the Salt and Gila Rivers allowed the Phoenix Basin Hohokam to fill miles of canals. Farmers in other basins used floodwaters in tributary streams after heavy summer rains, along with smaller-scale canals, to water their crops. The Hohokam raised corn, beans, squash, and cotton in irrigated and floodwater fields. They also trapped surface runoff in stone grids, on low terraces, behind checkdams, and under mulches of piled rock on dry slopes to grow smaller amounts of these crops and to raise agaves for food and fiber (fig. 1.7).

Hohokam Historical Trajectories
The beginnings of agriculture in Hohokam country

at about 2000 BCE kicked off a rise in population and an increase in societal complexity that would span the Hohokam millennium. The arrival of domesticated corn, or maize, from Mexico curtailed the seasonal movements of the hunters and gathers who had populated the Sonoran Desert before this time. By 1500 BCE, early cultivators in the Tucson Basin were constructing irrigation ditches in small settlements along the Santa Cruz River. Archaeologists find many large food-storage pits in and around the small, circular houses of these early farmers. Along with the substantial labor invested in building canals and maintaining fields, stored harvests suggest that people stayed in their settlements for much of the year.

An important transition in the organizational scale of society about 450 CE coincided with the consolidation of patterns in artifact styles, architecture, and economics that archaeologists define as

Hohokam culture. People came together in more permanent settlements with well-built pithouses. Homes surrounded central plazas in the largest villages. Soon, Hohokam people in the Phoenix Basin began to construct the massive irrigation systems for which they are famous. Hallmarks of Hohokam culture such as ball courts, red-on-buff pottery, palettes, and censers made their first appearances, and people began to cremate their dead, a practice common among the Hohokam. Ritual objects and ball courts signaling participation in Hohokam ideology reached their greatest regional extent between 700 and 1150 CE, a time span that archaeologists call the Hohokam Preclassic period. During the same interval, cultural developments in Chaco Canyon peaked, and Chacoan-style "outlier" settlements proliferated across the Puebloan Southwest to the north of the Hohokam.

The transition to the Classic period after 1150 CE marked a watershed in Hohokam culture. Phoenix Basin potters produced less and less of the trademark red-on-buff pottery and eventually stopped making it entirely in favor of pan-Southwestern styles. Rather than continue to arrange pithouses in small groups around a shared courtyard, villagers began to build larger groups of adobe rooms inside walled compounds. Toward the end of the Preclassic period, the Hohokam stopped building and using ball courts. Instead, as the Classic period opened, they began erecting platform mounds with rooms on top. Like the new adobe houses, the mounds were enclosed within a wall. They reflected a new set of rituals and beliefs that included the acceptance of a growing hierarchy among social groups. Local inhabitants built platform mounds in an area smaller than that over which ball courts had once been distributed. Canal systems in the Phoenix Basin, in contrast, reached their greatest extent, and cultivation away from the rivers increased. Most Hohokam subareas reached their maximum populations during the Classic period, while population densities increased at the largest centers. Puebloan people migrated from the north into the Hohokam basins, heightening the diversity of the occupants.

Sometime between 1400 and 1550 CE, Hohokam society collapsed, and the Hohokam disappeared as a coherent archaeological culture. Because archaeologists have found so little evidence for what really happened at the end, they hold conflicting opinions and promote different scenarios. The long record of large and sustained agricultural settlements within Hohokam boundaries ends without any clear transition to groups with new cultures. We have little information about the people of the Phoenix Basin until the Spanish Jesuit missionary Father Kino visited the area more than a century later, in the 1680s. By that time, indigenous peoples did not closely resemble the Hohokam.

One current scenario, based on reconstructions of annual Salt River stream flow from tree-ring data, sees disastrous fourteenth-century floods leading to unpredictable harvests, hunger, and disease, forcing many people to leave the region. According to another view, an increasingly hierarchical and demanding leadership fostered political instability and was overthrown from within. O'odham oral traditions describe events of this sort (see chapter 15). Other archaeologists propose that the deadly new diseases introduced into central Mexico by the Spaniards traveled rapidly along the trade routes, dealing a devastating final blow to the Hohokam.

Hohokam Archaeology and Archaeologists

A few pioneering Southwestern archaeologists came to Arizona in the late 1800s and early 1900s to excavate at major Hohokam sites for patrons and institutions in the East, but they did not maintain these interests throughout their careers. The first person to dedicate himself to studying the ancient people of southern Arizona was Harold Gladwin, who established his own research station, called Gila Pueblo, and went about defining the extent of the "Red-on-Buff culture" in the early 1930s. Lacking professional training as an archaeologist, he hired a young scholar named Emil W. Haury to assist in his excavations at Snaketown on the Gila River, the most influential of all Hohokam sites (map 2). The central importance of Emil Haury and his work to Hohokam archaeology cannot be overstated. During his long and distinguished career at the University of Arizona, Haury returned to Snaketown in the 1960s and later published a

Figure 1.8. Emil Haury looks down an excavated canal at Snaketown in 1964.

report that remains the classic reference for Hohokam studies (fig. 1.8).

A relatively small number of publications on the Hohokam appeared before the early 1980s, when a rapid change in the structure and personnel of Hohokam scholarship was just getting under way. A complex of new federal and state laws mandated that archaeological remains be inventoried and investigated before land could be developed (see chapter 13). University faculty and students were joined by archaeologists in growing numbers of private companies that formed to meet the demands of Arizona's dramatic urban growth and large-scale federal land and water projects. Federal, state, county, and city agencies and, finally, tribal

governments hired archaeologists and established programs to oversee threatened archaeological resources. In Arizona, the Bureau of Reclamation and the Arizona Department of Transportation were major funders of Hohokam research, sponsoring large projects and a continuing series of smaller efforts. An explosion of publications resulted in the following decades. In just 25 years, the Hohokam domain became one of the most intensively studied regions in the world, and scholars now must scramble to absorb the exponentially expanding archaeological data.

The contributors to this book represent the dynamic mix of researchers and scholars that marks today's Hohokam archaeology. They speak to readers "from the trenches" as the archaeologists who have designed and directed some of the most innovative and insightful research of recent years. Chapter authors include university faculty, owners and principal investigators of archaeological companies, and scholars at nonprofit archaeological centers. They also are federal agency archaeologists, tribal archaeologists, tribal cultural resource managers, and tribal elders. Together, they represent a diversity of expertise, experience, and viewpoints that hardly could have been envisioned a few decades ago.

Suzanne K. Fish and Paul R. Fish are both curators of archaeology at the Arizona State Museum and professors of anthropology at the University of Arizona. Suzanne Fish's research in the Arizona-Sonora borderlands involves ethnobotany, traditional farming, archaeological settlement patterns, and Hohokam social and political organization. Paul Fish's Hohokam research emphasizes settlement patterns, farming systems, and the emergence of complexity.

Figure 2.1. Dan Arnitt maneuvers a backhoe to carefully remove soil covering Hohokam pithouses.

Hohokam Beginnings

two

Henry D. Wallace

As Dan Arnitt skillfully guided the massive, six-foot-wide metal blade attached to the business end of his Case backhoe across the loose sandy soil, Mike Lindeman and I watched (fig. 2.1). We knew that he was uncovering one of the earliest sedentary, or permanently settled, villages in the American Southwest, but we didn't know whether the large soil stain he had begun to expose marked the location of a single prehistoric pithouse or several of them. We had already discovered one large square structure and a number of large rectangular ones at the site, and at first, when Dan's backhoe blade exposed another large, clearly square stain, we didn't think much about it—just another pithouse.

Before about 1150 CE, the inhabitants of southern Arizona built their pit dwellings so that the floors lay as much as two feet below the ground surface. When people abandoned their houses or destroyed them by fire, others living nearby filled them with refuse, or else the pits filled up naturally with the dark soil and debris of a long-occupied settlement. These types of fill left a clear difference in soil color for us to see as Dan scraped the backhoe blade across them. We knew so little about the time period when this village was occupied that we could not predict its layout. But a few days later, when our crew had excavated enough of the square structure to reveal that its doorway opened onto what we had theorized might be a central plaza, the significance of what we had uncovered hit home. This village in modern Tucson was arranged around a central plaza, with several large, square houses facing inward along its sides, a pattern recognized

so far only at Snaketown, the most famous Hohokam site.

What we had found was key to understanding the origin of the Hohokam. Massive canal systems, sprawling villages, crafts such as figurines, trade goods from western Mexico such as copper bells and pyrite mirrors, and a seeming lack of prior developmental history led Emil Haury to conclude that the Hohokam had migrated from the south with their distinctive culture already full-fledged. In 1976, when this preeminent Hohokam scholar published his classic work *The Hohokam*, he proposed that these people brought irrigation technology and trade contacts with them from what is now Mexico. Other archaeologists thought that the Hohokam developed from some ill-defined earlier population or that they were later immigrants who displaced earlier inhabitants. During the 1990s, a string of large-scale excavations in the floodplain of the Santa Cruz River in central Tucson (map 1) began to turn these ideas on their heads.

Santa Cruz Bend, Los Pozos, Las Capas, and Stone Pipe—all sites that were unknown until the 1990s—are playing a leading role as archaeologists piece together the origins of the Hohokam. We now know that people lived along the rivers of southern Arizona for a very long time before the Hohokam era. They grew corn, also known by its native name, maize, by 2000 BCE. Corn, beans, squash or pumpkins, and other Hohokam crops came to the American Southwest from Mexico, where the earliest farmers domesticated them from ancestral wild plants at least 6,000 years ago. Arizona farmers began

Figure 2.2. An aerial view of the small, excavated pithouses of early irrigators shows post holes and storage pits on many floors.

to irrigate maize crops by 1500 BCE, when small groups of farmers using relatively short canals inhabited settings favorable for irrigation in the floodplain of the Santa Cruz River. They lived in small, impermanent settlements of circular huts similar to Apache wikiups. Made of bent poles, the houses probably sheltered their makers for only one or two seasons. The farmers may have moved with the seasons, spending summers near their crops and moving to other locations for wild foods during the rest of the year. They repeatedly cultivated the most favorable stretches of the river, leaving behind the remains of hundreds of now buried dwellings at some sites.

Viewed from afar, the excavated house foundations in these long-used places look as if someone went wild with a set of cookie cutters—loads of little round pithouses surrounded by little round outdoor pits for storage and other purposes (fig. 2.2). The marine shell beads and pendants found in these sites are clear precursors to similar sorts of artifacts

that show up later in Hohokam settlements. In short, the earliest agricultural settlements along the Santa Cruz River mark the beginning of a long developmental sequence leading up to the cultural patterns we identify as Hohokam.

It is not difficult to see, however, why Emil Haury thought that the Hohokam were immigrants from Mesoamerica. Little evidence for pre-Hohokam people exists around modern Phoenix, the future heart of Hohokam territory and scene of the earliest research on this ancient civilization. Almost all of the evidence for its origin comes from other drainage basins farther south, primarily near Tucson. But there is one more piece to our puzzle, a piece that archaeologists still know little about. After the widespread preceding occupations by early farmers, why do we largely lose sight of them for nearly four centuries?

The riverside settlements of the early agriculturalists that I have just described drop out of the picture around the beginning of the common era, 2,000 years ago. The only signs we have of the people who followed the early farmers date from about 50 to 450 CE, encompassing what archaeologists call the Early Ceramic period. These signs consist of a few small settlements and a few isolated structures found at sites where people still lived in later times. At the start of the Early Ceramic period, around 200 CE, the Santa Cruz River and perhaps other drainages in southern Arizona cut deep channels that would have made filling canals difficult, if not impossible, and left existing systems high and dry. It was not a good time to be a farmer.

The Early Ceramic period is so named because at this time we begin to see the regular use of pottery for containers and storage. Before this time, and as early as 1300 BCE, we find small pots that did not serve everyday uses. The people of the Early Ceramic period situated their settlements higher on the margins of the floodplains than did earlier residents. They also built larger, more substantial structures. At first these were circular, as in preceding centuries. Then, around 350 CE, residents began to build small rectangular structures with roofed entries.

The hard times of the Early Ceramic period might well have led Tucson farmers to move north to become the first settlers and canal builders in the middle Gila and lower Salt River valleys. In a twist of fate, the deeply cut rivers farther south might have accelerated the development of permanently settled life, the rise of the Hohokam, and the emergence of the Hohokam cultural core in the Phoenix area. Certainly no archaeologist before the 1990s could have guessed that a catastrophe in Tucson might have given birth to Phoenix!

What transformed the small, relatively short-lived agricultural hamlets and farmsteads of the Early Ceramic period into the long-lived villages and towns of the Hohokam, with central plazas, ball courts, and later ritual and civic architecture? Rephrased, the question becomes, Why did the first villages form? Archaeologists have often assumed that once farmers in both the Old and New Worlds began irrigating high-yield crops, the decision to settle down in villages followed naturally because people needed to protect their heavy investments in

canals and fields. The problem is, archaeological evidence does not always bear out this assumption.

In the realm of the Hohokam, we find evidence of the primary crops and extensive irrigation more than a thousand years before we find signs of the first long-term, fully sedentary villages. Archaeologists call this in-between time the Early Agricultural period, but I think of it as the time of people's living together without living together. It was a blend of the older, mobile, hunter-gatherer life-style with a farming existence that tethered cultivators to one spot on the landscape for months at a time. Long-term settlement brought with it new social problems. It is much easier to get along with neighbors if you can move away when relations sour. But early farmers could move only short distances from their irrigated fields, going out to hunting and gathering camps for parts of the year. Periodically, perhaps at harvest time, everyone came together, sharing labor, seeking spouses, and exchanging goods. But this was not village life, and the politics and rituals that go with packing diverse social groups together were not yet necessary.

Some anthropologists have long argued that cramming people into villages and towns is costly and will persist only if benefits outweigh the costs. Residents must be willing to tolerate lines of authority, community rules, increased exposure to diseases, and unpleasant neighbors. In return, they get security through strength in numbers and the adjudication of property, water, and irrigation disputes. In southern and central Arizona, a critical set of conditions was in place by 475 CE: sustainable irrigation agriculture, populations that had expanded into most of the farmable land along the rivers, and the know-how to construct lasting settlements. What pushed them over the threshold to permanent village life?

When I began to work at Valencia Vieja in 1997, no one had ever excavated a large portion of a village dating to the beginning years of the Hohokam sequence. The only clues to village plans of that age came from the very large site of Snaketown, which Emil Haury last excavated in the 1960s. When David Wilcox later reanalyzed the plan of Snaketown, he recognized that very large, square structures oriented at right angles to one

Figure 2.3. Backhoe trenches reveal the locations of pithouses and the village plan at the Valencia Vieja site, in the foreground.

another faced onto Snaketown's large central plaza and these were not the homes of ordinary residents. Too little was excavated at Snaketown, however, to reveal how the rest of the village looked when the early square structures were in use. Excavating at the humble Valencia Vieja site, most of which probably could have fit inside the enormous plaza at Snaketown, Mike Lindeman and I hardly expected to duplicate Haury's earlier findings—but sometimes you find what you least expect.

The fortunate day began with one of those warm, sunny January mornings that Midwesterners dream about. We had designed our preliminary excavations at Valencia Vieja to sample carefully a selection of the houses we had discovered, by placing backhoe trenches across the site (fig. 2.3). We chose a handful to excavate fully in a part of the site where investigations would be limited. We had just excavated one of these, which turned out to be a very large, square structure facing onto what might be a central plaza. As Mike and I watched a crew member expose the entry of Feature 53, another unusually well-constructed large square structure, Mike pointed out that its entry, too, faced onto the possible plaza, at right angles to the one previously exposed. A few quick calculations, some lines drawn on the site map, and we determined that not only did these two dwellings face onto the plaza on the south and east sides, but also a third structure, tested earlier, similarly faced the plaza on the north. Of course, our thoughts immediately turned to Snaketown. Could this be a small version of the same pattern seen there? We began to suspect that the Valencia Vieja village plan held some surprises, a suspicion soon confirmed as additional structures were exposed.

What we ultimately uncovered at Valencia Vieja looked like nothing Hohokam archaeologists had ever seen before. Sometime around 425 CE, 5 to 10 households, loosely arranged along a low terrace above the river floodplain, had founded the settlement. It probably was no larger than the typical settlements of times past. We can infer from the site's setting that the best spots along the river were already taken and that the Valencia Vieja farmers had to construct new canals to water their fields.

Around 500 CE, not long after the beginning of the initial Hohokam period—aptly named the Pioneer period—Valencia Vieja doubled in size with an influx of newcomers. It suddenly became a small village. In short order, the residents established a plaza in the center of the community, and by 600 CE they had built as many as eight large square structures (fig. 2.4) flanking the plaza. These structures probably housed the leaders of the separate lineages or clans that came together to live at the site. Unlike other houses, each leader's house (fig. 2.5) had one or more tiny huts next door that would have accommodated no more than a single adult on a temporary basis. Additional homes of the leader's kin were smaller than the leader's and rectangular rather than square. They were situated around small courtyards behind the leader's home and away from the plaza. Each of these extended families also had a square structure away from the plaza that served as a workshop and held ritual paraphernalia. The leadership position likely was hereditary. A successor in line for the leadership role—presumably a child of the leader's—was probably the resident of an additional square structure near the leader's house but smaller and farther from the plaza.

What we found at Valencia Vieja was a village very much in transition. The village as a whole still showed signs of the way it had been pieced together from the original kin-group segments. Politically, this pattern suggests village rule by a council.

Why did people come together? Mike Lindeman and I believe that two forces pushed people toward village life. The first was eminently practical: many hands are needed to build large canals, and everyone who participates has a stake in the land the canal irrigates. Pooling labor would have been most critical in the Salt River valley when people began to extend the massive irrigation canals far from the river for the first time. The second factor was the potential for conflict over land and water. A land rush was under way in the fifth century CE (fig. 2.6). Every canal built by a kin-group co-op laid claim to land and water that others could not use. Combining forces was a good way to ensure property and water rights. I believe that people

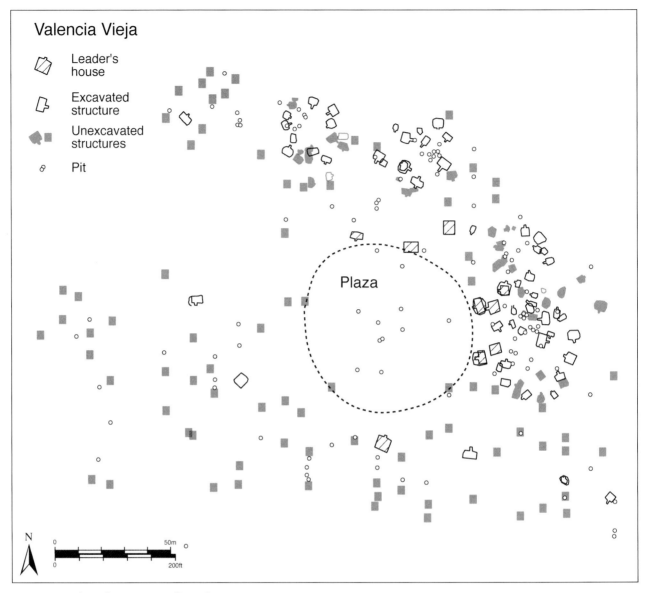

Figure 2.4. The Valencia Vieja village plan.

would not have chosen to create villages without this pressure. Once residents built substantial houses and developed canal systems, villages were largely locked into place.

Throughout the Hohokam region, many other groups established villages at about the same time as Valencia Vieja and Snaketown, and they continued to occupy most of them for hundreds of years. Once established, such villages generated new values and rules of social interaction that had been unnecessary before. More than anything, villages created the need for members to feel a collective identity tied to the village, as well as affiliation

with their individual kin groups. In the beginning, the Hohokam solution was similar to that seen in ancient societies of the Near East, Mesoamerica, and the Caribbean: they constructed plazas in the centers of the villages and buried revered ancestors (or human remains symbolizing them) there. Plazas were public stages where shamans and leaders (sometimes one and the same) could perform and officiate at events and rituals that helped bind a community together. Burying the ancestors in the plaza also served to tie people to one place on the landscape and to one another. Many archaeologists believe that the small clay figurines dating to the

Figure 2.5. The exposed floor of a leader's large house that opened onto the plaza at Valencia Vieja.

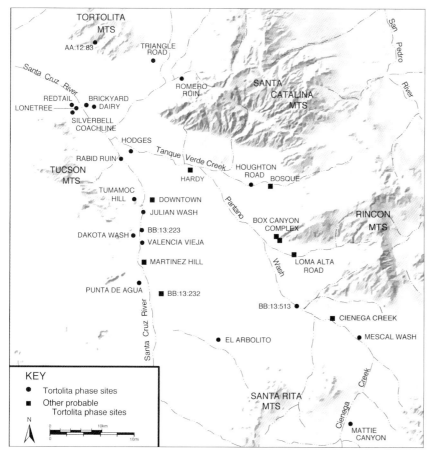

KEY
● Tortolita phase sites
■ Other probable Tortolita phase sites

Figure 2.6. By the time of Valencia Vieja (450–650 CE, or the Tortolita phase), farmers had settled throughout the Tucson Basin.

seventh century CE represent ancestors and show that ancestor worship was part of the beliefs of this early Hohokam village era (fig. 2.7).

The changes we discovered during our excavations at Valencia Vieja detail the development of a Hohokam cultural identity over the two centuries from 500 to 700 CE. The distinctively Hohokam red-painted pottery, which formerly had been very rare, became commonplace. Developing architectural styles were unique to the Hohokam area. Nowhere else in the Southwest had village residents organized themselves the way people did in this region. We can safely say that the beginning of the Hohokam archaeological culture corresponds to the appearance of plazas, sometime around 500 CE, when the key elements of a Hohokam tradition had come together.

By that time, potters were producing a greater diversity of vessels that could be used for a wider variety of purposes, including, most importantly, cooking. The ability to routinely cook foods such as stews would have permitted the preparation of soft foods and therefore the early weaning of children. Women who stopped breastfeeding infants earlier became fertile again more quickly and could bear more children. In short order, improvements in stone implements for maize grinding appeared on the scene, perhaps in concert with the new flour corn varieties, which improved the nutritional value and ease of preparation of the staple food. Together, these changes

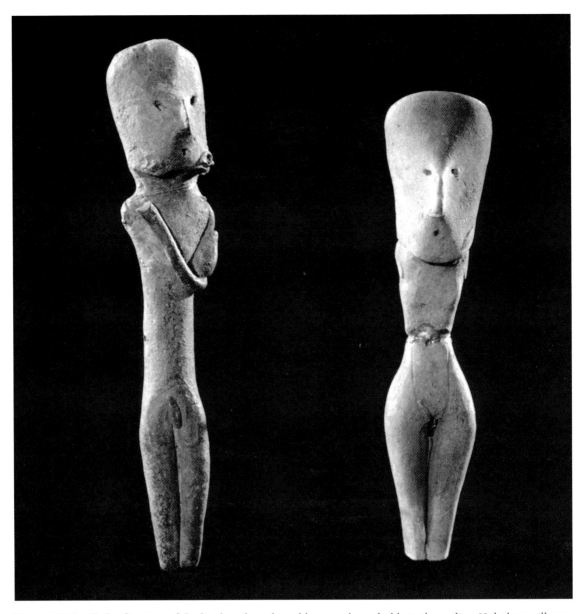

Figure 2.7. Small clay figurines of the kind made and used by most households in the earliest Hohokam villages.

in technology and cuisine fostered population growth.

We know only a little about the religious and ceremonial lives of early Hohokam villages, but there are clues. The plaza burials and numerous, standardized clay figurines strongly suggest some form of ancestor worship, which is common in developing societies. Rituals and ceremonies that continued from earlier times likely focused on irrigation cycles, planting and harvesting times, and the desire for abundant summer rain. Some of the figurines wear what appear to be the arm and thigh

pads of ballplayers, indicating that residents might have played a Mesoamerican-type ball game in the plazas at this time, even before the construction of the first Hohokam ball courts.

I returned to Valencia Vieja in 2004, some six years since our excavations there. As I stood on the edge of the parking lot that now covers part of the site and looked out across the remaining, untouched village, I could not help wondering what other surprises lay beneath the desert sands. Insights into the way villages are founded, why people choose to live together, and what happens when they do—all this and more came from the work at this unassuming early site. As I turned to head back to my dusty truck, I wondered whether the first few families who joined forces and moved in together at Valencia Vieja had any idea that they were changing their culture forever.

Henry D. Wallace is senior research archaeologist with Desert Archaeology, Inc., in Tucson and has directed many Hohokam excavations in the Tucson and Tonto Basins. His research focuses on the Hohokam Preclassic period, village organization, ceramic studies, and iconography.

Figure 3.1. Hohokam faces modeled in clay between about 900 and 1150 CE.

Growing Up Hohokam

Patricia L. Crown

Today Hohokam villages are silent and often difficult to find. To catch glimpses of the men, women, and children who lived there, archaeologists must locate the crumbled homes and clear them of dirt and debris. They uncover, clean, and fit back together broken Hohokam artifacts. Specialists help identify food remains from the animal bones, pollen, and charred plants preserved in these elusive sites. Yet a thousand years ago, these same villages teemed with life: babies cried, children argued over games, teenagers dressed in finery to attract the opposite sex, and adults labored to support their families. How do archaeologists bring those villages to life again? What can we say about what it was like to grow up in a Hohokam village?

Archaeologists have many resources with which to reconstruct the lives of the Hohokam. Excavations provide abundant information about houses, outdoor areas, tools, and food remains. Burials, painted and sculpted images, and community structures such as ball courts and platform mounds provide evidence of beliefs. Skeletal remains reveal information about diet, disease, causes of death, population structure, and even workloads. By combining this information, we can say much about Hohokam culture.

Describing Hohokam lives requires moving from the material world of the archaeologist to the lived world of actual people in the past. In doing so, we are somewhat restricted to those aspects of life that leave material traces, especially traces that withstand the destructive forces of time. To fill in the gaps, we rely on historical writings and observers' ethnographic accounts of the Native American groups who lived in the Hohokam area when Europeans arrived. And when necessary, we consider cross-cultural regularities seen in peoples around the world to reconstruct the Hohokam past.

For example, many archaeologists assume that women made the pottery vessels found in the Hohokam area. Why? First, early ethnographic and historic descriptions of ceramic production in this area indicate that women were the primary pottery producers, although men sometimes painted pots made by their mothers, wives, or sisters. Second, worldwide cross-cultural comparisons show that traditional, hand-built pottery made for use in the household is almost always made by women, whereas wheel-thrown pottery made for sale is nearly always made by men. Third, the few pre-Hispanic Southwestern images that depict people making vessels are of women. Finally, Southwestern burials that contain potters' tool kits are those of adult females. I am confident, therefore, in assuming that almost all the people who made Southwestern vessels were women, but not every Hohokam archaeologist would agree (see chapter 8).

If reconstructing past lifeways is so difficult, why even try? I believe that everything else we study about the Hohokam, from canals to ball courts, becomes more interesting when we know about the lives of the people who created, used, and discarded the material remains we find. Such knowledge permits us a more active view of the past and fills it with real people. Furthermore, reconstructing past lifeways is one of three major goals of archaeology as a profession, along with reconstructing cultural histories and studying processes of culture change.

We cannot study past lifeways without taking into account how human societies are divided along lines of age and sex and how the lived experiences of individuals varied according to age, sex, and status. In addition, archaeologists are just discovering that different child-rearing practices are tied to different rates of culture change, so reconstructing childhood may be particularly useful for understanding why some cultures change slowly and others change rapidly. Finally, it is particularly satisfying to look at the past in new ways and to search for those aspects of culture that leave the subtlest evidence. For instance, archaeologists have always known that there were children in Hohokam villages, but we are only now developing methods to distinguish the material traces they left behind from those of their adult relatives.

In describing what it was like to grow up Hohokam, I collapse the myriad lived experiences of thousands of individuals into a single hypothetical life. Imagine trying to describe what it is like to grow up in the United States on the basis only of what would be preserved as material remains. We might say that babies are born in special community structures (hospitals); children attend community educational centers from ages 5 to 18; training there includes reading, writing, and arithmetic but rarely how to cook, hunt, farm, or make tools; formal education is mostly by direct instruction from specially trained adults; people are adults when they marry and have families; and people die in special community structures (hospitals or hospices) away from their homes. This would not be true for everyone, nor would it approach the richness of individual lives. Furthermore, it ignores the important changes in life-styles that have taken place during the almost 250 years since this country was founded.

Just as each of our lives has distinctive characteristics, so did the lives of each Hohokam. What follows, then, is a generalized view of Hohokam life, grounded in what we know from the material world of the Hohokam and most accurate for the Hohokam Preclassic period, from about 700 to 1150 CE. I use a life history approach to structure the story, beginning with birth and ending with the death ritual. As you read, keep in mind that this is informed speculation, and insert *probably* or

likely or *most individuals* wherever you think appropriate.

Hohokam Childhood

When labor began, a pregnant Hohokam woman went to a special birthing hut built near her own house or in a nearby field. Tended by experienced women, the mother gave birth. No men entered the hut. After remaining in the birthing hut with her infant for a few days, the mother emerged to introduce the newest member of the community. Historic documents describe the use of such birthing huts by later Native Americans living in this area, and the remains of small huts in Hohokam villages suggest that this practice has great time depth.

Hohokam children had many relatives in their villages, so parents, aunts, grandmothers, and older siblings all helped care for small children. Mothers nursed infants, adding mashed squash and cornmeal gruel as the child accepted solid foods and gradually weaning the child to the traditional diet of domesticated crops, wild plants, and the meat of rabbits, deer, and other wild animals. From tooth analysis of infant skeletal remains, we know that mothers weaned children at two and a half to four years of age. Infants and young children wore only ponchos fashioned from small blankets with a slit in the center for the head (fig. 3.2).

Once children could walk, they spent their days in groups of village children, watched by the older girls. Girls and boys played in a village filled with working adults going about their chores. Adults might ask children to help with some activities, such as fetching water or tending a younger sibling, but most of childhood was unstructured. When children became interested in learning adult tasks, they watched and imitated adult relatives of the same sex. Boys practiced hunting with small bows and arrows; girls made miniature pottery vessels and baskets. Eventually, girls and boys were drawn into such daily domestic tasks and spent less time at play. Their lives thus diverged as they matured, each learning the appropriate activities and behaviors expected of them as adults.

My own research concerns the way children learned to become competent potters among the

Figure 3.3. Mistakes in painting and laying out patterns show the early stages in a child's learning the craft of pottery.

Figure 3.4. A pottery scoop shows the poorly controlled painting of a child.

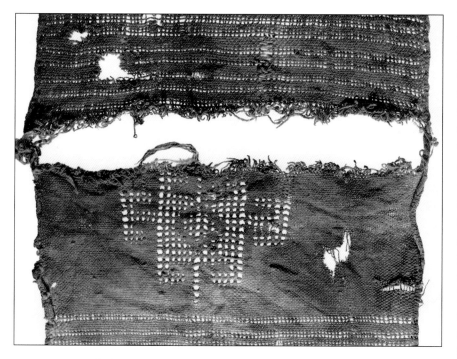

Figure 3.2. A Hohokam child's cotton poncho.

Hohokam and other Southwestern groups in the past. I examine poorly made and painted vessels and evaluate them using techniques developed by educational psychologists and art therapists who study the drawing and sculpting abilities of children (figs. 3.3, 3.4). Judging by the complexity of the designs and the competency of the motor skills reflected in ancient pots, Hohokam girls began learning to make pottery by the age of 10. They worked alongside skilled adult potters, watching and imitating their actions. Southwestern Native American parents rarely gave verbal directions on how to do something,

but they did offer a critique
after the child finished the
task. Through observation and
imitation, children gradually
attained mastery of the many
tasks involved in making and
painting a pot.

Skilled Hohokam potters
formed vessels by first building
up their shape with fat ropes
of clay. They then thinned and
shaped the vessel wall by holding a mushroom-shaped stone
anvil on the inside while slap-
ping the clay rolls on the outside and opposite the anvil
with a small wooden paddle,
like those used today for piz-
zas (fig. 3.5). Girls did not
initially make pots using a
paddle and anvil; rather, they
formed the clay with their hands or molded it in
existing bowls into smaller versions of the shapes
made by adults. Sometimes adults made vessels and
allowed children to decorate portions or all of them.
The girls learned to paint a fairly rigid set of standard designs. It appears that adults emphasized and
guided Hohokam children into doing things the
"right way," for little creativity or innovation appears
in the girls' designs and there are relatively few
errors. Interestingly, this may be responsible for what
we know about the Hohokam ceramic sequence: that
it is characterized by slow, gradual changes in design
on a stable technological foundation.

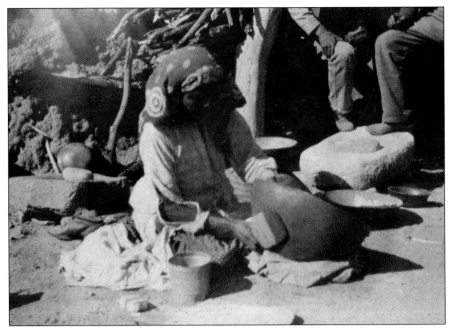

Figure 3.5. A Tohono O'odham potter of the late nineteenth century uses a paddle to
flatten coils of clay into the smooth walls of a jar.

Hohokam Adolescence and Adulthood

Judging from figurines, tools included in burials,
and historic accounts of Native American groups
who occupied the Arizona desert, archaeologists
believe that the Hohokam had a rigid division of
labor. Women processed and prepared food, gathered wild food, crafted pottery and baskets,
processed and spun fiber into thread, and tended
children. Men hunted, crafted their own hunting
tools, went on salt-gathering and trading expeditions, and served as warriors. Both men and women
trapped small game, farmed, wove textiles, dug

canals, and constructed houses. On the basis of
what we believe are protective pads for ball games
on male ceramic figurines, it was men who played
the ball games. This does not mean that women
never fought or that men never cooked meals, but
the Hohokam conducted most activities along lines
of gender and age.

We do not know whether the Hohokam held
puberty ceremonies, but historical records and
archaeological discoveries of very small structures
on the edges of villages suggest that during men-
struation, girls and women lived in seclusion in
segregated, special-purpose huts. There they had
separate dishes and blankets, likely because men-
struating females were considered dangerous to the
larger community. Boys and girls might have been
initiated into religious societies, including, for boys,
rituals surrounding the ball game. Hohokam society
assumed that all children would master the gender-
appropriate skills needed to run a household by the
time they were of marriageable age, which was at
the onset of puberty, or about 14 to 16.

After marriage, Hohokam men and women
spent most of each day laboring to produce and
process food, create the tools needed for household
tasks, and fashion clothing, blankets, and orna-

Figure 3.6. An Akimel O'odham woman of the early twentieth century grinds corn kernels by pushing a stone mano across the surface of a metate, catching the flourlike meal in a basket.

ments. Villages bustled with activity. Families had some privacy within household structures and courtyard areas, but the open layouts of Hohokam villages during the Preclassic period encouraged interaction. Gathering, farming, and hunting probably occupied part of every day, and some types of food preparation involved long hours of repetitive work. This was particularly true of grinding corn on stone metates with stone manos held in the hand. Every female in a family helped grind corn as soon as she was able (fig. 3.6).

Households were largely self-sufficient. However, a few skilled persons acted as part-time specialists, producing crafted objects beyond the needs of their own household to exchange for food, other goods, or services such as labor or curing. This was especially true for ceremonial objects, such as slate palettes and stone or pottery censers. Some people acted as part-time ritual specialists as well. Men acted as curing shamans or herbalists, while women—probably mostly postmenopausal women—served as shamans, herbalists, or midwives. Men also primarily took on leadership positions, although oral traditions recorded historically in this area include women in roles of power. Women probably held such positions of leadership relatively rarely and after menopause, when monthly seclusion was no longer an issue.

In the warm southern Arizona desert, clothing was unnecessary much of the year. Evidence from figurines and ceramic decorations suggests that men and women rarely wore much clothing. Historically, men wore breechclouts, and boys usually adopted these after age 10. Occasional figurines are depicted wearing breechclouts, and archaeological evidence indicates that these were made of bundled string or strips of cloth attached to belts. Female figurines are nude, but archaeological evidence suggests that women sometimes wore string aprons or bundled strings that passed between their legs and were attached front and back to a belt. Everyone owned a blanket. On cooler days, Hohokam people wore their blankets over their shoulders or wore short fur robes that fell to the waist. It is possible that women sometimes wore blankets folded and tied around the waist as short skirts, as was true historically. Sleeveless shirts woven into lacey gauze might be worn for ceremonial occasions. Footgear consisted of sandals, probably worn only on the hottest days to protect the soles of the feet from the scorching desert.

Historically, men in this area wore their hair in what we would now call dreadlocks, fashioned with mud and decorated with cotton strings, feathers, and other ornaments. On special occasions they wore headbands wrapped around the hair on top of the head to form a turban. Figurines prove that turbans and headbands were common for Hohokam men as well (fig. 3.7), although whether they wore their hair in long dreadlocks is unknown. Depictions of males sometimes show feathers worn vertically or protruding horizontally from their hair. Archaeologists recover large, carved, bone hairpins that were used to hold hairstyles in place (fig. 3.8). Historically, women in the area wore bangs and cut their hair as a sign of mourning. Hohokam women may have worn their hair short, an inference made because figurines and effigy pots (vessels made as representational images) of women generally lack any indication of hair.

Body adornment was common. Human figurines and human effigy vessels show jewelry, piercing, and body decoration (plates 3 and 4). As in the case of hairstyles, male figures show the more elaborate body adornment. Men commonly wore

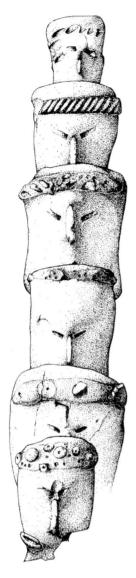

Figure 3.7. Preclassic figurines showing hairstyles, headbands, and turbans.

Figure 3.8. Carved bone hairpins decorated with the common Hohokam motif of a bird eating a snake.

necklaces, often with three strands. Thin bands on upper arms may be shell bracelets, whereas thicker bands on upper arms and legs may represent padding used in ball games (see fig. 5.1; plate 11). Anklets appear on some male figurines as well. Many male figurines show ear pendants, plugs, or spools. Some have a perforated nasal septum as well, and this form of body decoration is corroborated by the discovery of nose plugs of stone, shell, and wood in Hohokam sites. A few male figurines have red body paint, and some have paint or incised designs on the face. These may represent tattooing or less durable painting. Figurines of women who are not pregnant often have red stripes on the abdomen, whereas those representing pregnant women do not. Perhaps body painting served as an indicator of fertility. Female figurines rarely display jewelry, except for ear pendants or ear plugs.

Hohokam society respected older persons. As their strength and pace declined, older men and women spent more time in the village, creating crafts and tending children. They often took on leadership roles within the community.

Hohokam Death

At death, the body was cremated. Survivors dug an elongated pit, placed wood in it, put the body and associated offerings on top of the stacked wood, and set the wood on fire. Typically, they then collected the cooled ashes and bone fragments and buried them with offerings in a pit or placed them inside a ceramic jar, which they buried in a pit. The bones of one person were sometimes placed in multiple pits. Sometimes the cremated remains were simply left where they were burned. Rarely, survivors buried the dead without cremation during the Preclassic period, before 1150 CE. Inhumation, or the burial of intact bodies, would become the norm during the later Classic period. In such instances, mourners generally placed the bodies in pits on their backs with their legs extended and their heads to the east.

If someone died inside a Hohokam house, survivors might have burned the house and its contents, as was done in this area historically. Alternatively, they might have used the timbers from the deceased's home to create the funeral pyre. Survivors burned items with the bodies of the deceased, but no set group of objects was consistently cremated with every body. Common categories of items found with cremations include pottery vessels, arrowheads, shell and bone ornaments, and stone palettes. Charred traces of textiles and sandals are occasionally preserved as well. From these remains, archaeologists suggest that survivors placed bodies that were clothed and wore jewelry, along with utilitarian objects such as dishes, stone food-grinding tools, and hunting tools, on the funeral pyre. Finally, they sometimes included items that likely were used in the funeral ritual, such as stone palettes and stone or ceramic censers.

The types of grave offerings differed by sex, but most items were probably the personal effects of the deceased. Grave offerings placed with adult females were primarily utilitarian objects such as pottery and cooking implements, whereas offerings placed with adult males included hunting implements and, more frequently, ornamental or ritual objects. Persons aged 10 to 20 often had the richest burials, marked by large quantities of shell ornaments, bracelets, and beads. Although this might reflect the importance of this age group as future producers for the society, it might simply indicate the importance of finery to youths of marriageable age.

With the warm climate and abundant resources of the desert, we might expect that Hohokam life was idyllic. Yet during the later Classic period, when inhumation rather than cremation was the rule and complete skeletal remains are available for study, at least some Hohokam villages experienced high mortality rates for infants, children, and teenagers. At the large site of Pueblo Grande, few people lived beyond 50. Frequent patterns denoting nutritional stress, including anemia, characterize the inhabitants of this village as well.

An infant born in a Hohokam village grew up in a very different way from an infant born in the United States today. Hohokam culture persisted with little change for a thousand years, whereas our culture is changing so rapidly that we have to explain to our children what life was like before computers, cell phones, and iPods. Even the stable and distinctive Hohokam culture eventually became altered beyond recognition and was replaced by different ways of living and growing up. The dynamic villages fell silent as the Hohokam moved to other places and other lives. Now, their inhabitants become vital beings once again through the work of archaeologists.

Patricia L. Crown is professor of anthropology at the University of New Mexico. She has worked extensively with Hohokam remains along the Gila River and at the time of this writing was directing an excavation project at Chaco Canyon. Her research interests include gender studies, iconography and ideology, subsistence systems, and ceramic analysis.

Figure 4.1. Aerial view of pithouses and courtyard groups exposed by excavations at the Grewe site (see page 32).

Houses, Households, and Household Organization

four

Douglas B. Craig and T. Kathleen Henderson

Dams now impound the mighty rivers that once filled the largest irrigation works in ancient North America, and their courses run dry. Most traces of the people who built and maintained the canals and whose villages stretched from one end of the Phoenix Basin to the other have disappeared as well. A few fragments of broken pottery, an occasional chipped stone tool, or bits of shell jewelry on the surface of the ground are often the only markers revealing where a Hohokam village once stood. Everything else has been destroyed, plowed under, or covered over by asphalt and concrete.

Appearances can be deceiving, though, as archaeologists found out in the late 1970s when they started probing beneath the surface of modern, metropolitan Phoenix. Much to everyone's surprise, once the layers of dirt and asphalt were stripped away, thousands of well-preserved features from Phoenix's distant past emerged into view. The remains of Hohokam houses, in particular, seemed to be everywhere. Although these houses were small and unimpressive by today's standards—most were one-room pole and brush structures covered with hardened mud (plate 8)—they have provided archaeologists with a wealth of information. Much of what we currently know about Hohokam domestic life, for example, is based on the analysis of artifacts and preserved bits of food found in and around the houses. We also now have a much better idea how Hohokam villages were internally organized, as a result of studies of the spatial arrangement of houses within settlements.

Courtyard Groups and Households

A key study in this regard was David Wilcox's reanalysis of house data from the site of Snaketown. In *Snaketown Revisited*, published in 1981, Wilcox observed that groups of houses from the same time period often were arranged around a common open space, or courtyard (fig. 4.2). He attributed this pattern to the presence of extended family or multifamily households that shared resources and pooled labor for joint undertakings. Wilcox suggested that these groups of related houses, known as "courtyard groups," were the primary social units in Hohokam society—not individual houses, as previous researchers had thought. Most of the courtyard groups he identified at Snaketown contained two or three houses all used at the same time. He also identified several large courtyard groups that contained up to six contemporaneous structures. The appearance of these large courtyard groups during the last period of Snaketown's occupation signaled to Wilcox the possible emergence of elite households.

Many of the ideas that Wilcox advanced in *Snaketown Revisited* gained widespread acceptance over the following 25 years. Archaeologists have now identified courtyard groups at sites throughout the Hohokam region. Most researchers have followed Wilcox's lead and equated courtyard groups with household-level social groups whose members were related through kinship. Although we cannot reconstruct the exact size and composition of these social units from the archaeological record, ethnographic patterns among Southwestern Native

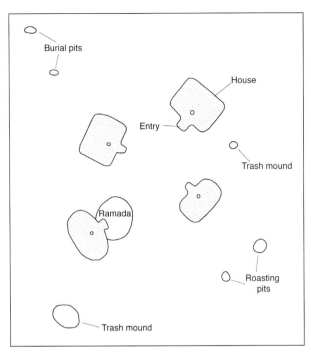

Figure 4.2. Plan of an idealized group of four pithouses with a shared central courtyard, roasting pits, and a designated area for trash disposal.

American groups suggest that a nuclear family—a married couple and their children—formed the household core (fig. 4.3). Yet the composition of individual Hohokam households undoubtedly varied, just as households vary today. Some households must have been large and included extended family members (grandparents, siblings, aunts, uncles, cousins), as well as nonfamily members (friends, laborers). Others probably consisted only of the nuclear family.

Reflecting such differences, Hohokam courtyard groups varied considerably in size and components. For example, as part of recent excavations at the Grewe site—the village ancestral to Casa Grande Ruins in south-central Arizona—we identified about two dozen courtyard groups in a residential district bordering the site's central plaza (fig. 4.1). The smallest courtyard group contained only two houses and covered about 1,100 square feet, whereas the largest contained 26 houses and covered more than 6,500 square feet. Typically, only one or two houses were occupied at any given time, but

Figure 4.3. A Tohono O'odham household of the late 1800s, including a couple, their children, and an additional relative.

this number rose to five or six in the largest court-yards (plate 21). Judging from house sizes, we estimate that households averaged 5 to 10 members over time, but at their peak a few households might have boasted 20 members or more. The variability in courtyard groups seen at Grewe is not unique. Similar ranges have been reported from Preclassic villages across the region. Relative to courtyard groups at many other sites, however, some of Grewe's were uncommonly large in terms of the space they incorporated.

Our research at Grewe further showed that Hohokam courtyard groups varied in their lengths of occupation. Some were occupied for one or two generations, and others for several hundred years. Additionally, only rarely did we find courtyard areas built over earlier house groups or disturbed by succeeding ones. This length of residence in one place is impressive by nearly any standard. We view it as evidence that courtyards belonged to someone—namely, the household unit—and that rights to the property were transferred across generations. Houses and their associated courtyards were presumably among households' major possessions. Also, because courtyard groups first appeared among farmers who irrigated, it stands to reason that household holdings included fields and garden plots along canal systems. This supposition is consistent with what is known about self-governing irrigation societies throughout the world. Cross-cultural studies have shown that the household usually acts not only as the primary institution for regulating cultivated land in irrigation communities but also as the primary social unit for passing agricultural holdings to succeeding generations.

Field Houses and Farm Land

Evidence that Hohokam households held irrigated land comes from a recent archaeological project at Phoenix's Sky Harbor Airport. The airport sits on the floodplain adjacent to the Salt River, and in the past farmers used the site primarily for irrigated fields. In this agricultural landscape, researchers on the Sky Harbor project found pairs of contemporaneous large and small "field houses," structures built alongside fields for convenient use during agricultural

work (fig. 4.4). The larger houses usually contained a hearth and were rectangular with rounded corners in outline, whereas the smaller ones lacked a hearth and were oval to circular. The presence of hearths indicates regular indoor cooking or heating. The form and contents of the larger houses suggest that they were seasonally occupied dwellings, with the smaller structures serving for storage or other specialized purposes. In several cases, an outdoor storage pit near the paired structures suggests another component of the field house complex.

We also found several field houses built over one another or situated so close to one another that they probably were used sequentially. The overlapping houses fit the characteristics of dwellings. Although their casual construction showed that they were meant for less permanent use than the houses in nearby villages, the replacement of earlier field houses implies long-term commitment to the same field location. Just as the rebuilding of houses in village courtyard groups illustrates the persistence of those households, the sequential replacement of field houses in the same location tells us that they served ongoing households.

Sets of paired field houses appear repeatedly over time in the Phoenix area—not only at Sky Harbor but elsewhere along the Salt River. They suggest that Hohokam farmers followed a cultural template for the way field house complexes were supposed to be organized. Together, evidence for the long-term use of fields and the organization and renovation of buildings convinces us that field-house complexes were the seasonally occupied farm buildings of households that lived in village courtyard groups.

The establishment of permanent villages along the Gila and Salt Rivers coincided with the construction of the first large-scale canal systems. Households that participated in canal building might have been able to select the most productive irrigable land for their fields, as was the case among the Akimel O'odham, or Pima, who succeeded the Hohokam along the Gila River. Later arrivals might have had to choose from less desirable remaining tracts. In turn, greater access to prime irrigable land might have set the stage for "first-comer" households to gain wealth and status through productive success.

Figure 4.4. At Phoenix's Sky Harbor Airport, excavated field houses are visible along the path of a pre-Hispanic canal, indicated by dashed lines.

Household Wealth and Status

Some degree of economic inequality exists in all human societies. But many preindustrial societies deploy social sanctions that encourage sharing and prevent individuals and households from acquiring "too much" inappropriate wealth. Random events such as crop failures and inheritance disputes can also reduce accumulated wealth. Unfortunately, the kinds of data used by most social scientists to establish differences in wealth—such as tax rolls and landownership records—do not exist for the kinds of societies that archaeologists typically study. Archaeologists have to look for proxy, or substitute, measures of wealth that can be applied to a broad cross section of the population, much like a census report today.

In an effort to address the issue of Hohokam economic inequalities at the Grewe site, we again focused on architectural data, partly because of the large sample of houses we had to work with, but also because of the nature of the site. As a result of

modern farming in the area, only those prehistoric features that lay deeper than the reach of a plow remained. Even where plow scars damaged the floor of a house, careful excavation often revealed the details of its construction. But plowing tended to damage or scatter artifacts, so we rarely recovered intact sets of original artifacts from the houses. Our best chance for investigating differential wealth patterns for a large segment of the population was to use information about architecture, not artifacts.

Another reason we focused on architecture was that cross-cultural studies had shown that wealthy households, in the past as in the present, typically live in larger, more ornate dwellings than do poor households. To see whether this was the case at Grewe, we first developed a method for estimating the amount of labor required to build each house, a method based on a combination of archaeological and experimental data. We then looked to see where the most labor-intensive—that is, the most costly—houses were located, as well as when they

Plate 1. Shells with etched designs are limited to the Hohokam Sedentary period (900–1150 CE).

Plate 2. Turquoise mosaics on whole carved shells are rare artifacts that may have indicated the status or office held by the wearer.

Plate 3. Male human effigy pot dating to 900–1150 CE, with pierced ears, pierced nose, painted or tattooed face, lizard pendant necklace, upper arm bands or bracelets, and painted designs of probable cotton clothing.

Plate 4. Female human effigy pot dating to about 900-1150 CE, with pierced ears, painted or tattooed face, and painted designs of probable cotton clothing.

Plate 5. Hohokam red-on-buff and plainware pottery of the Preclassic period.

Plate 6. Salado Polychrome pottery of the Hohokam Late Classic period (1300–1450 or 1500).

Plate 7. Artist's reconstruction of the platform mound and adobe residential compounds at the Marana Mound site.

Plate 8. A modern reconstruction of Hohokam-style pithouses sharing a common courtyard, in an exhibit at the Gila River Indian Community Cultural Center.

Plate 9. Artist's reconstruction of the Pueblo Grande platform mound in Phoenix.

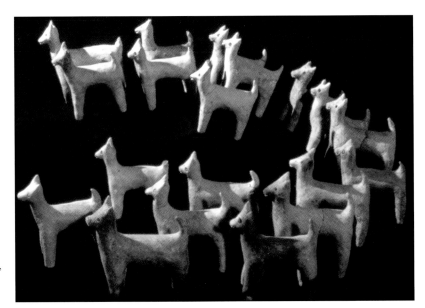

Plate 10. Residents of Snaketown during the Sedentary period (900–1150 CE) buried this set of ceramic animal figurines, which likely represent deer.

Plate 11. Pre-Hispanic ceramic model of a ball court, ballplayers, and spectators from Nayarit, Mexico.

Plate 12. Aerial view of Mesa Grande, one of the two largest Hohokam platform mounds, engulfed by urban development.

Plate 13. Aerial view of the ball court at the Redington Ruin in the northern San Pedro Valley.

Plate 14. A canal at the Gila River Indian Community still waters fields in the vicinity of Snaketown.

Plate 15. Bases of adobe walls mark the outlines of a Classic period compound during excavations at the Marana Mound site.

Plate 16. Archaeologist Bruce Masse examines the cross sections of two intersecting Hohokam canals exposed in the wall of a backhoe trench. The larger one, on the left, is a later replacement of the canal on the right.

Plate 17. Aerial view of public architecture at Casa Grande Ruins National Monument, with roofed "Big House" (lower left), ball court (center), and compound enclosing two platform mounds (upper right).

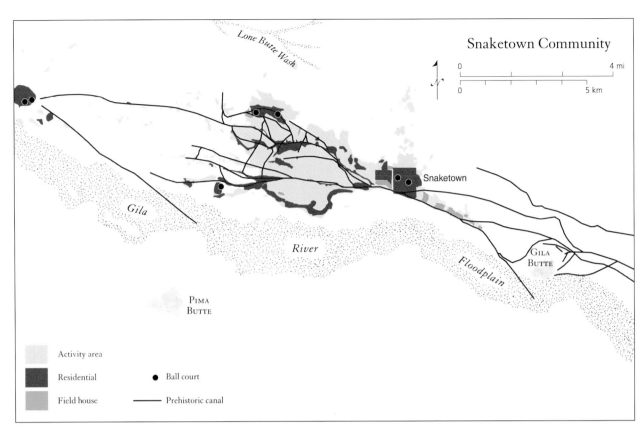

Plate 18. The consolidated Snaketown-Santan irrigation community.

Plate 20. Tire tracks show the impressive scale of a well-preserved segment of this Phoenix canal.

Plate 19. Aerial view along the San Pedro Valley.

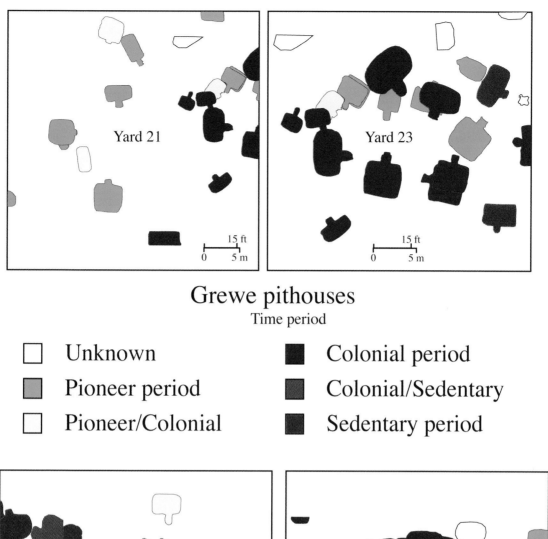

Grewe pithouses
Time period

☐ Unknown   ■ Colonial period

■ Pioneer period   ■ Colonial/Sedentary

☐ Pioneer/Colonial ■ Sedentary period

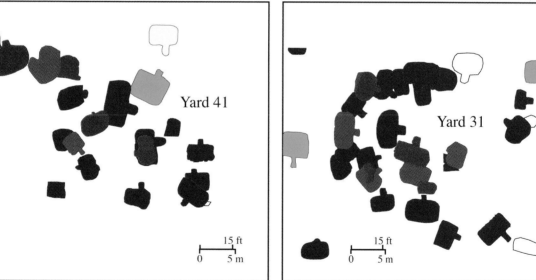

Plate 21. Successive pithouses in each of four courtyard groups at the Grewe site are color-coded by period of construction and use. The surprising discovery that courtyard groups persisted sometimes for hundreds of years was a breakthrough in Hohokam archaeology.

Plate 22. Tohono O'odham women gathering organ pipe cactus fruit, as drawn by botanist Arthur Schott in 1854.

Plate 23. Following Tohono O'odham tradition, Juanita Ahil gathers ripe saguaro fruits in early summer in the 1960s.

were occupied. Interestingly, we found that most of the "expensive" houses, which cost more in terms of labor investment, were clustered in only a few courtyard groups. We also found that the courtyard groups with expensive houses were the ones that tended to be occupied the longest. We view this as evidence that wealthier households at Grewe were able to maintain their advantage across several generations. It follows that the development of an effective household strategy for maintaining and perpetuating property was an important first step in the emergence of permanent forms of inequality in Hohokam society.

A question that naturally arises in light of these findings is what role wealthier households played in the social and political transformation of Hohokam society. Were households key political players whose heads competed for power and positions of village leadership? Or were households supporting actors with little influence beyond the domestic realm?

The evidence from Grewe comes down squarely on the "household as key political actor" side of the debate. On the basis of the discovery of a communal cooking area with dozens of pit ovens (*hornos*) cut into the earth, we believe that one way wealthier households at Grewe acquired power was through the control and performance of communal rituals, particularly rituals connected to the construction and use of ball courts. On one side of the communal cooking area was a residential district with hundreds of houses arranged into courtyard groups; on the other side was a public plaza containing a ball court. Although we are unable to link specific hornos or sets of hornos to specific courtyard groups, it stands to reason that the nearest groups, including the two wealthiest ones at the time, controlled the communal cooking area and sponsored feasts involving its use. Sponsoring households presumably gained prestige and status by hosting the gatherings and displaying generosity. Feasts might also have served as occasions to reaffirm property rights, thereby reinforcing the advantages already held by the wealthier sponsors. Feasting that took place in conjunction with ballcourt events likely contributed to a sense of civic pride as well.

Besides sponsoring feasts, wealthy households at Grewe may have subsidized craft production. Among the crafts Grewe residents produced and traded to people at other sites in the region were stone tools, pottery, cotton textiles, and shell jewelry. Not all households, however, took part in making and distributing these items. We found craft tools and raw material waste from craft production in only a few of the courtyard groups we investigated, and most of those were small courtyards situated on the margins of those occupied by wealthier households. In contrast, the residents of wealthy courtyard groups had more finished products and more exotic items from distant sources. One possible explanation for this pattern is that the small, craft-producing households at Grewe were attached in some way to the wealthier households, perhaps exchanging craft items for access to irrigated land or surplus food.

Regional Variability

Many of the patterns we have discussed for households in the Phoenix Basin find parallels in other parts of the Hohokam region. Most notably, archaeologists have found courtyard groups almost everywhere they have looked, as would be expected if the extended family or multifamily household was the norm in Hohokam society. But we are still trying to sort out one potentially significant difference that involves the length of time courtyard groups were occupied in different Hohokam areas. From what we can tell at present, relatively few courtyard groups at sites outside the Phoenix Basin were inhabited for more than one to three generations, perhaps indicating that maintaining the same kind of "estate" was less a concern for households living in those areas.

Evidence is also mounting that the persistence of courtyard groups may be related to stability in landscape use. More changeable courtyard groups may be related to a corresponding instability. For example, even though Hohokam people in the Tucson Basin irrigated their fields with water from the Santa Cruz River, they frequently moved village and household locations short distances to accommodate shifts in the river's channel and changes in its floodplain. In contrast, the Gila River floodplain

Figure 4.5. Successive pithouses built in the same location indicate the long-term stability of courtyard groups and villages along the Salt and Gila Rivers.

was relatively stable for much of the 600-year occupation of the Grewe site (500–1100 CE), providing households with reasonable assurance that they could cultivate the same plot of land year after year. Greater residential stability in both courtyard groups and villages would be expected under such conditions, and in fact that is what we find (fig. 4.5). In the 1800s, the Akimel O'odham used irrigation methods similar to those of the Hohokam to farm virtually the same stretches of the Gila River. Just as prehistoric village locations had shifted in the Tucson Basin, the locations of O'odham villages tended to shift because the Gila floodplain had become less stable by the nineteenth century.

The Key Role of Households

Understanding households is central to understanding Hohokam society. Indeed, the more we

learn about Hohokam households, the more impressive their accomplishments appear. Not only did their members build and maintain a highly sophisticated network of irrigation canals, but they also provided most of the labor and skill to sustain an intensive agricultural economy for close to a millennium. For many years, archaeologists attributed the success of Hohokam households to a combination of hard work, mutual cooperation, and developmental duration. Renowned archaeologists such as Emil Haury and Richard Woodbury argued that even canal systems as large as the Hohokam networks could have been built in small segments by a few dozen households working together over many years. These scholars further maintained that all Hohokam households were similar and that differences in wealth and status between households were small and short-lived. Survival in a harsh desert environment supposedly dictated that everyone work together and pool resources for the common welfare.

A very different perspective on Hohokam households has emerged in recent years. This new perspective reflects a belief on the part of a new generation of scholars that many Hohokam households were property holders with a vested interest in maintaining their proprietary rights through time. Independent households apparently held claims to plots of land and passed them down from one generation to the next. In contrast, the entire community probably held rights to water for irrigation and allocated them to households according to the amount of land each had under cultivation. There can be little doubt that households sharing water rights also shared an interest in protecting those rights and their investment in canal infrastructure. Some degree of cooperation and coordination among households was clearly necessary to maintain the canal system and ensure its continued operation.

The extent to which households shared in other collective, or corporate, ventures is less clear. According to the anthropologist and historian Thomas Sheridan, peasant farmer communities generally value household autonomy and view cooperative ventures as a "necessary evil, not a desired goal." Reflecting this concern, they typically limit collective control to specific tasks and resources that households cannot manage on their own. Thus, self-interest often goes hand-in-hand with collective action, and communal institutions are often less a source of power than a means of legitimating power relationships that already exist.

We envision that a similar dynamic tension between private and collective interests existed in southern Arizona in Hohokam times. Indeed, such an interplay, in which neither interest conclusively won out, might have provided a balance that enhanced the long-term stability of Hohokam society. At the same time, major social changes took place between the Preclassic and Classic periods. Until recently, most archaeologists attributed these changes to "macro-processes" beyond the control of individuals, such as natural disasters and large-scale migrations. But as convincing evidence for these "macro-processes" has failed to materialize, researchers increasingly turn their attention to the cumulative consequences of "micro-processes" that shaped everyday life in Hohokam society. As the social unit most closely tied to everyday life, households provide a crucial link in understanding the cumulative effects of these underlying processes.

Douglas B. Craig is a principal investigator with the Central Arizona Division of Northland Research in Phoenix. For the past 25 years he has conducted Hohokam research in all regional subareas. His published studies emphasize architectural expressions of social organization, political economy, and the changing character of the household. T. Kathleen Henderson is a project director with the Phoenix Office of Desert Archaeology, Inc., and has worked continuously in the Hohokam region for the past 20 years. Her research specialties are settlement structure analysis, social organization, and chronology.

Figure 5.1. A set of large ceramic male and female figurines dating to the Colonial period (750–900 CE) shows details of Hohokam dress. Turbans and pads on the upper arms of some of the males resemble the garb of the ballplayers shown in plate 11.

Community, Territory, and Polity

Paul R. Fish and Suzanne K. Fish

If archaeologists could travel back in time to the Hohokam millennium, many of us would eagerly ask the first Hohokam people we encountered, "Who are you?" We would hope for a layered reply that listed the various ways they identified themselves and were identified by their contemporaries. Their answers would reveal what anthropologists call "social identity," or where individuals stand in relation to the important social divisions and institutions of their society.

Most archaeologists already have ideas about how a Hohokam person might answer this question, based on the customs and traditions of descendant peoples such as the O'odham (see chapters 14 and 15). The patterns we find in the archaeological record offer clues about Hohokam social identity too. What we know suggests that the people the time-traveling archaeologists met would likely respond that they belonged to an immediate family and to an extended kin group that linked older and younger generations. A Hohokam might further offer that he or she belonged to one or the other of two broad divisions of society (moieties) that together included all members. He or she might also belong to a special-purpose group such as a religious or military association whose membership crosscut the other social divisions.

We also expect that Hohokam men and women would tell us about affiliations based in their ties to particular places. They might begin by mentioning that they were part of a household that owned a small group of pithouses (see fig. 4.2), if they lived during the Preclassic period (700–1150 CE), or that they were members of a walled adobe compound enclosing multiple households (see fig. 10.6), if they lived during the later Classic period (1150–1450 or 1500). They almost surely would identify themselves as residents of a particular village with its adjoining land. By looking at the spatial patterning of sites, archaeologists have concluded that Hohokam people also had a civic affiliation beyond their own village. This larger unit of population and territory consisted of a prominent central village containing communal buildings—ball courts or platform mounds—and an outlying set of smaller villages and farmsteads, along with the cultivated and natural areas surrounding all these settlements. Archaeologists call these multisettlement Hohokam units "communities." We believe that belonging to such a community was a fundamental part of Hohokam social identity and that learning about communities is equally key to our archaeological understanding of the Hohokam.

Defining Hohokam Communities

Archaeologists' use of the word *community* for a Hohokam central village with ball courts or platform mounds and a related set of outlying settlements is a specialized usage. It differs from the meaning of the word in everyday English, that of a single locale and its residents, who share common concerns. The archaeological term *community* reflects the same essential meaning, however, in that residents of each Hohokam settlement in the closely related set shared the same community identity and interacted according to commonly held rules and beliefs. We believe that leaders in the central villages coordinated communal affairs by directing

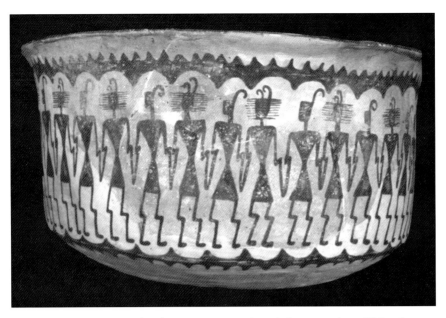

Figure 5.2. Dancers encircle a large serving vessel made between about 900 and 1150 CE, probably representing some sort of community gathering.

munities, because the remains of these relatively massive buildings are still visible or were documented before they were destroyed. Most pithouses and even adobe houses are harder to locate. More to the point, today's sprawling cities and large-scale, mechanized agriculture have wholly obliterated many small Hohokam settlements.

A useful analogy for the size and arrangement of a Hohokam community is that of a modern county of the small size typical of the eastern United States. The county courthouse and possibly a few other public buildings are located in the county seat, which also contains the larger churches and the commercial district and hosts the county fair. Individual towns in the county are autonomous in many respects, but officials at the county seat coordinate and regulate countywide affairs. The distribution of county courthouses would serve as a handy proxy for the distribution of county seats and their associated counties. Similarly, the distribution of centers with ball courts or platform mounds serves as a good proxy for the locations of Hohokam communities. The distribution of these monuments even serves as a proxy for the extent of Hohokam culture at a given time because these buildings were designed for distinctively Hohokam ideological and ritual practices.

Archaeologists did not always recognize community patterns of settlement in the archaeological record of the Hohokam. Early investigators either targeted single sites or pursued questions on a grand geographic scale—for example, identifying the boundaries of Hohokam culture by mapping the regional extent of its trademark red-on-buff pottery. In the 1970s, David Doyel offered a pioneering definition of a segment of Hohokam society that encompassed multiple settlements. He reasoned that an irrigation network branching from a single river intake connected a constellation of interde-

civic and ritual events at ball courts and platform mounds on behalf of all community members (fig. 5.2). Whether the bonds of community were primarily political, ritual, or economic is still an open question, but all these social factors tend to be intertwined in the roles of leaders and institutions in societies that are less complexly organized than states. Most archaeologists do not think that the Hohokam lived under a state-level government, because we see no evidence for all-powerful rulers backed up by force or well-developed administrative bureaucracies (see chapter 1).

How do archaeologists recognize communities and other divisions in Hohokam society? The divisions of a society are likely to be reflected in the organization and use of space, so archaeologists search for spatial patterns as clues. They look for recurring elements in similar positions relative to one another and for continuity in these patterned relationships over time. For example, in chapter 4, Douglas Craig and Kathleen Henderson describe the patterned placement of pithouses in arrangements called courtyard groups. The public buildings in central settlements (ball courts in the Preclassic period and platform mounds in the Classic period) typically provide the starting points for locating and determining the layouts of com-

pendent villages whose residents must have shared the efforts of canal construction, maintenance, and management and who must have found a way to ensure the peaceful allocation of water rights (see fig. 1.1). He called all the archaeological sites united in this manner an "irrigation community"—a higher-order unit than a ball court or platform mound center and its outlying settlements. As many as six such communities and their surrounding territories are spaced along the longest of the canal networks in the Phoenix Basin.

David Wilcox's subsequent concept of a "ball court community" highlighted relationships among settlements that define a more basic kind of Hohokam community. Building on an idea first suggested by the renowned Hohokam scholar Emil Haury, Wilcox established the important role of centers with ball courts in Hohokam settlement and society. At the centers, people from surrounding areas could gather for ball games between villages, hospitality and feasting, trade, and social interaction. As Wilcox noted, ball court sites are relatively evenly spaced along large irrigation networks, so we can draw community boundaries approximately midway between adjacent centers. Several of the shortest canal lines in the Phoenix area have only one center with public architecture at their midpoint; in these cases, perhaps a single ball court or later platform mound community managed the irrigation network.

Another reason to consider the individual ball court or mound-centered community a fundamental Hohokam approach to organizing settlements, people, and territory is that such communities appear in the landscape even where no major irrigation networks exist. Outside the Phoenix Basin, Hohokam irrigation was of a decidedly smaller scale, but archaeologists see the same pattern of settlements clustered around central sites. When we systematically surveyed more than 700 square miles of the Tucson Basin, we found several separate and clearly bounded clusters of settlements surrounding centers with public architecture. Canals linked a minority of the settlements in these communities or none at all. Even where Tucson communities included irrigated land along a river, the center with public buildings was not always located in this zone. Some communities were not even situated

adjacent to a river. Finding the community pattern of settlement outside the heavily irrigated Phoenix Basin tells us that the demands of water management in huge canals did not alone determine the way the Hohokam organized themselves to live together. Rather, it must reflect widely shared Hohokam ideals.

Reconstructing Community Relationships
Although the layout and spacing of communities tell us a great deal about how the Hohokam structured their collective lives, these patterns only indirectly reflect the civic practices and beliefs that instilled a sense of belonging and unity in the members of Hohokam communities. Relationships among Tohono O'odham settlements, first recorded in the 1860s, offer valuable insights into the social workings of Hohokam communities. In the sort of settlement group that the anthropologist Ruth Underhill called a "village unit," the founding village had a mother-daughter relationship with the other settlements in its group. This main village had a ceremonial house and a foremost ceremonial leader who presided even when other leaders took the stage. Outlying residents obeyed the officials of the mother village and returned to it for major events (fig. 5.3), even when their own daughter settlements grew large enough to have their lesser leaders and ceremonial houses. In intervillage games, members of all settlements belonging to the village unit played and bet on the same side. In the early 1930s, Underhill observed that "the loyalty of each individual is, above everything else, to his village and its partners."

In a similar way, a web of civic, political, social, economic, and ritual relationships probably united the members of Hohokam communities. We cannot rely exclusively on the traditions of contemporary O'odham people for the answers to questions about the Hohokam, because much has changed since Hohokam times. Nevertheless, similarities are apparent between O'odham village organization and that of the Hohokam.

Our long-term research in the northern Tucson Basin brought home to us the rich network of relationships that forged Hohokam community life. The Early Classic period (ca. 1150–1300) Marana

Figure 5.3. A Tohono O'odham participant in an early-nineteenth-century Vikita ceremony, jointly celebrated by all the settlements in a village unit. Compare with the pre-Hispanic dancers in figure 5.2.

Community, named after a nearby modern town, covered about 56 square miles, crossing all basin environments between mountains on either side (figs. 5.4, 5.5). Community territory beyond the bounds of the villages provided everyone with access to wild plants, game animals, firewood, and raw materials for building houses and making tools and crafts. Depending on where their fields lay in the basin, community farmers cultivated them by irrigating from the river, diverting storm flow from tributaries, or trapping overland runoff after rains. In the better-watered fields they grew mostly corn, beans, squash, and cotton. On dry slopes they tended plantings of drought-resistant agave for food and fiber. Fields in the full variety of environmental settings across the community meant that poor harvests in some fields could be offset by better results in others. For example, trade and sharing could help even out food supplies when rainfall was spotty in

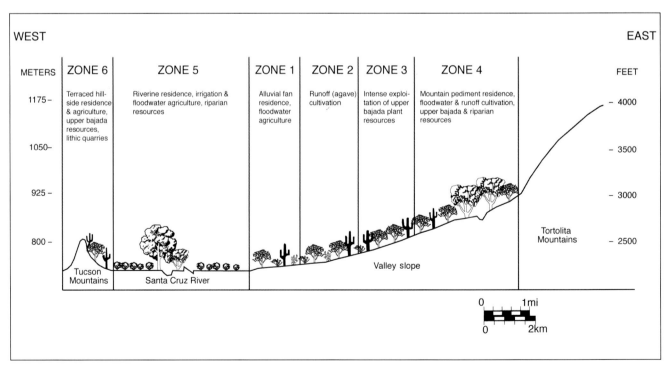

Figure 5.5. Cross section of the northern Tucson Basin showing residential and agricultural zones within the Marana Community.

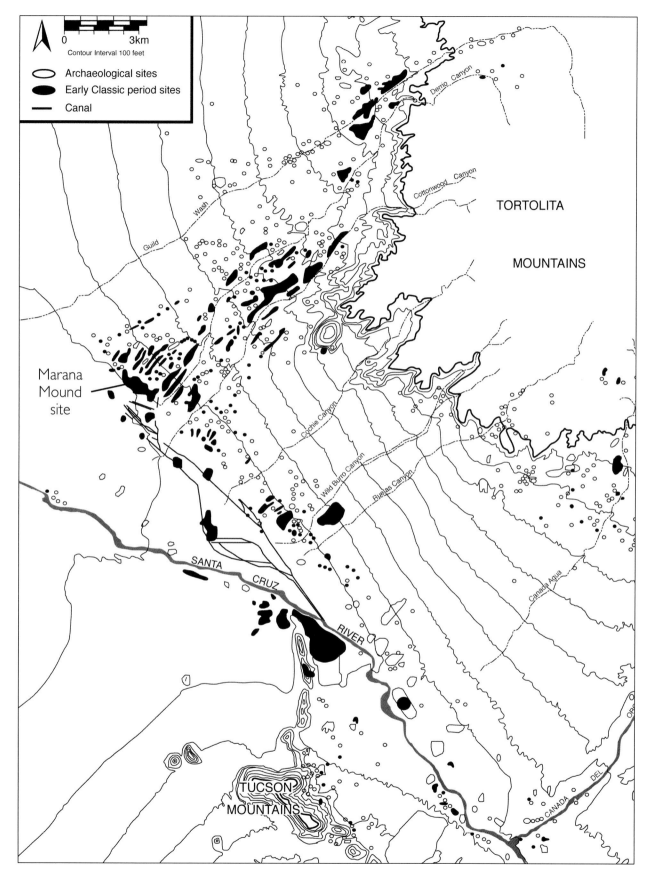

Figure 5.4. Settlements in the Early Classic period Marana Community, north of Tucson.

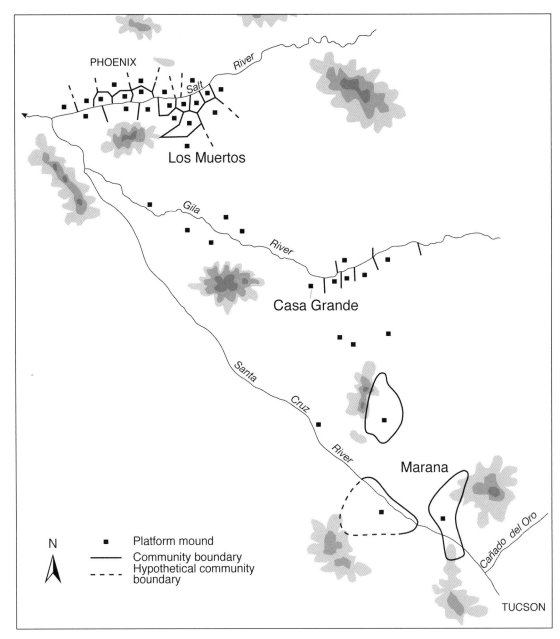

Figure 5.6. Approximate boundaries of Classic period Hohokam communities in the Phoenix and Tucson Basins.

fields on basin slopes or when river floods destroyed floodplain crops.

The Classic period Marana Community emerged when the settlements of two earlier and smaller ball court communities, one on the eastern basin slopes and one along the river, merged as they increased in number and size. The combined community grew as people moved into it from elsewhere in the Tucson Basin. The total area of Classic period residential settlements in the com-

munity grew rapidly to 2.3 square miles, tripling the total of the earlier two communities. Adobe rooms within 35 to 40 walled compounds at the new Classic center, the Marana Mound site, housed an estimated 800 to 1,000 residents, accounting for as many as one-third of all community members.

This large site with a platform mound occupied a strategic central position for coordinating the exchange of goods (plate 7). Community members exchanged cultivated and wild products from

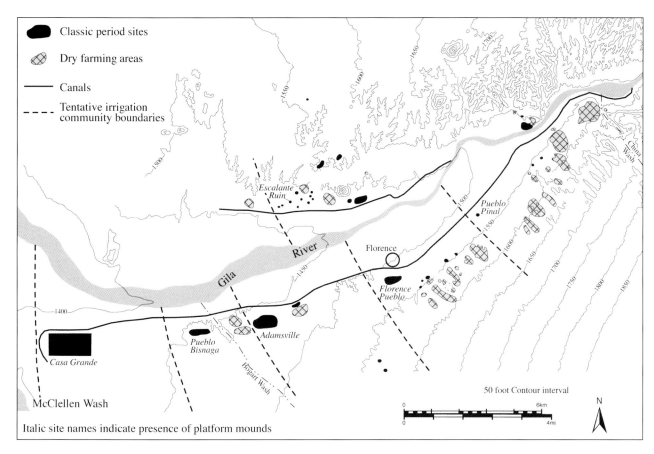

Figure 5.7. Approximate boundaries of Classic period communities along the Gila River south of Phoenix.

the community's different environments, as well as a variety of textiles, shell ornaments, and other crafts manufactured most intensively at the community center itself. Leaders living at the platform mound village enjoyed the advantages of its centrality. They were well positioned for rapid communication and prominent roles in trade and in communal rituals and feasts at the platform mound. Such centralized public events likely served to integrate newcomers from other parts of the basin into community life.

Comparing Hohokam Communities

Hohokam communities varied in size, and their territories presented different farming opportunities (fig. 5.6). On the Gila River south of Phoenix, communities ranged along single canal lines that paralleled the river downstream on either side (fig. 5.7). In each community, members cultivated large tracts of irrigated land next to the river. They

raised additional crops in non-irrigated fields and gathered wild resources in outer zones. Patricia Crown estimates that individual Gila community territories averaged 15 square miles and contained 2,550 irrigated acres.

On the Salt River in the location of today's urban Phoenix, canals diverged from the river and repeatedly branched as they crossed the broad basin floor. Irrigated land occupied most of this wide expanse. Dividing all basin floor land among all platform mound centers (fig. 5.8), Suzanne Fish estimates that Classic-period Phoenix Basin communities averaged 15 square miles, a striking match with Crown's estimate for Gila River communities. However, the more closely spaced Phoenix communities nearest the Salt River tended to be smaller and to have poorer access to non-irrigated land and wild resources than the larger communities on the edges of the basin. David Gregory and his colleagues estimate a total of 52,000 irrigated acres for

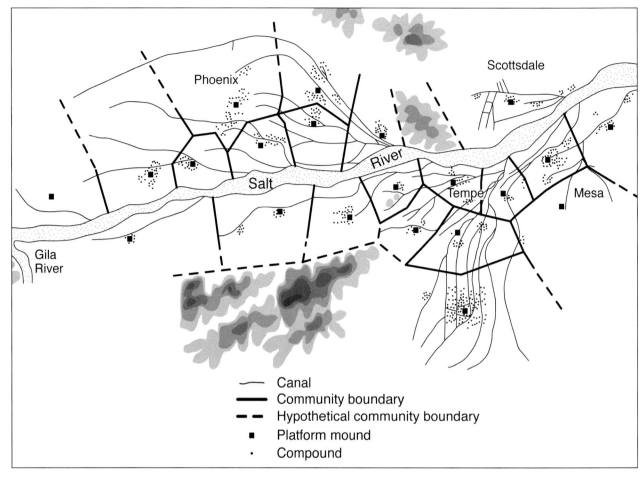

Figure 5.8. Approximate boundaries of Classic period communities along the Salt River in the Phoenix area.

all the Salt River canal systems. Again dividing this total by the number of platform mound centers, the average of 2,300 acres per community closely approaches the average for communities on the Gila River. If Hohokam farmers supported their families on the same amounts of land that historic Akimel O'odham (Pima) farmers used, then individual communities on the Salt and Gila Rivers could have raised enough food to support 2,300 to 5,800 members, bracketing our estimate of 2,400 to 3,000 persons for the Marana Community near Tucson.

The residents of Hohokam communities looked to leaders in the centers who coordinated ball court or platform mound events and other communal affairs. In this sense, communities appear to have had some of the characteristics of polities, or political units. The irrigation community, the more inclusive entity that linked ball court

or platform mound communities along an irrigation network, must also have had centralized means to coordinate water management and resolve disputes, especially when water was scarce.

Some Hohokam scholars see hierarchical relationships among the communities sharing Phoenix Basin canal lines. They identify the more powerful communities by the greater sizes and numbers of ball courts and platform mounds at their centers. These preeminent centers are often situated at the ends of the canals, where the strong assurance of an equal share of water would have been crucial. They are occasionally located at canal intakes as well, a good position for controlling the down-canal flow. Some archaeologists have proposed that the largest and most architecturally elaborate Classic period centers, Pueblo Grande, Mesa Grande, and Casa Grande (map 2), may have dominated the largest combined community territories, possibly incorporating communities beyond their own canal networks. It is unclear, however, how overall leaders might have controlled these community aggregates. Perhaps collective councils or incipient bureaucracies played a role.

The Hohokam developed a versatile and enduring means of guaranteeing the benefits of stable social networks beyond the household and village: community organization. They reproduced it again and again throughout their desert domain.

Community organization was sufficiently flexible to accommodate the coordination needs of densely packed irrigators in the Phoenix Basin and to serve the more dispersed farmers of the settlement clusters in other Hohokam basins. Although there is still much we do not know about the workings of communities and how they interacted with one another, we increasingly can see their fundamental role in Hohokam society, social identity, and the key relationships of everyday life.

Figure 6.1. Artist's rendering of Hohokam dancers and musicians wearing costumes suggested by prehistoric art and artifacts.

Into the Earth and Up to the Sky

Hohokam Ritual Architecture

Mark D. Elson

From a distance the mound looked like a mirage, shimmering in the heat of the midsummer desert sun. I stopped walking and stared hard at this earthen mass rising above the horizon, wondering whether I was heading toward something real or an illusion. As I got closer, I could see that the mound was both real and large, covering an area of around 100 by 160 feet and rising to almost twice my height (fig. 6.2). Climbing to the top, I counted the remains of at least 10 rooms and probably more. Erosion, combined with illegal excavation by pothunters, had gouged a channel into the mound surface, more than a meter deep across the short axis of the mound. Using my trowel to face the side wall of this trench, I soon exposed the mound fill: layers of rounded river cobbles alternating with 8- to 12-inch-thick lenses of prehistoric trash, adobe, and silt.

The nearest source for the river cobbles was along Tonto Creek, several hundred meters away. Standing there, sweating heavily in the afternoon heat, it struck me that to build a mound this size would have required tens of thousands of cobbles, all hauled by hand from the creek and then mixed with tons of adobe. This was an impressive feat in terms of both the labor involved and the structural engineering needed to stabilize a feature containing more than 70,000 cubic feet of fill. Without a doubt, I was in a very special place. Standing atop the mound and looking out over the Tonto Basin, I could easily imagine being here 700 years earlier, listening to the rhythmic beat of the drum and the chant of human voices, watching masked beings dance on the top of the mound and in the plazas below (fig. 6.1). To the prehistoric people living in the Tonto Basin, such ceremonies were an extremely important part of being Hohokam. Like holy days in our own time, the same ceremony might have been repeated on the same night at the same time throughout much of the southern Southwest.

Ritual is one of the few true cultural universals. Along with language, music, and art, all human

Figure 6.2. Aerial view of the well-preserved platform mound within the adobe walls of its compound at the Cline Terrace site in the Tonto Basin.

populations have some form of ritual behavior. As we know from our own practices, ritual acts can vary widely, both within and between groups, but at base, we conduct rituals to convey a powerful message. Ritual initiates the young into the culture and integrates separate, and sometimes opposing, social groups into the larger whole. People often carry out rituals in special places, which can take many forms, from small, open, outdoor areas to massive, constructed buildings. Archaeologists call the structures in such special places "ritual architecture" and find that they served both as stages on which ritual performances took place and as symbols carrying culturally specific meanings to participants.

Anthropologists have studied religious practices for years, but because ritual is so deeply embedded in a particular culture, it often remains difficult for outsiders to understand. In tribal societies such as those that lived in the prehistoric Southwest, ritual was a part of almost all spheres of life; it was not clearly separated from the economic, political, and social realms. Ritual is also a critical component of "ideology," the body of concepts that tells us who we are and what we believe, enabling us to characterize ourselves as a defined group in opposition to all other defined groups. The complexity of ritual is particularly apparent to the archaeologist, who has the difficult job of deciphering what ritual was like in the past using primarily architectural remains and the artifacts left behind from people's ritual activities.

Hohokam Ritual Architecture
Many people know that the Hohokam were skilled artists and artisans who made beautiful shell jewelry, elaborately carved stone palettes, and fine red-on-buff pots. From the earliest days of archaeological research, we have studied Hohokam art to understand the technology, the aesthetics, and even the beliefs of these ancient people (see chapters 8 and 9).

Fewer people know that the Hohokam were also master builders and highly proficient engineers. They built mostly with wood, brush, and adobe. If river cobbles or other rocks were available, Hohokam builders sometimes mixed them with adobe. All these materials were readily at hand and well suited for the hot, dry, desert environment, but with the

exception of river cobbles, they seldom survive long enough for archaeologists to record them, much less for the public to appreciate them. So, unlike the stone buildings of the Hohokam's Ancestral Pueblo neighbors to the north, most Hohokam architecture has melted back into the desert. As a result, the Hohokam are known more for their crafts than for their constructions.

Yet examples of two types of Hohokam architecture, ball courts and platform mounds, *have* survived the ravages of time and can tell us a great deal about ritual behavior. To build these structures, Hohokam communities had to divert some of their members from subsistence-related tasks such as farming, hunting, and gathering wild plants—not a trivial decision in the harsh Sonoran Desert. They also had to organize people to perform heavy labor for long periods. Because neither ball courts nor platform mounds were essential for survival or even for the conduct of everyday life, the choice to invest significant time and energy in building them gives archaeologists important clues to the nature of Hohokam society. Hohokam people almost certainly built and used ball courts and platform mounds as part of their ritual activities.

Ball Courts
Archaeologists have recorded more than 200 ball courts at some 160 prehistoric sites in Arizona (see map 3). The Sonoran Desert hosts the majority of them, but we have found them in all types of environments stretching over an area of approximately 50,000 square miles, from close to the US-Mexico border in the south to the upper Verde River valley, almost 125 miles north of Phoenix, in the north. The pine forests and grasslands around Flagstaff in northern Arizona—the prehistoric territories of the Pueblo-related Sinagua and Cohonina cultures—host about a dozen ball courts. Most of them were built many years after those in the Hohokam heartland to the south, and we do not know precisely what relationship existed between the Hohokam and the Sinagua and Cohonina people. For these reasons, I exclude the northern ball courts from the following discussion of their meaning.

In the field, Hohokam ball courts appear as large, oval depressions with raised embankments

Figure 6.3. The large ball court at Snaketown. The utility poles in the right foreground provide a scale.

(fig. 6.3). They vary widely in size, depth, and orientation, so they elude easy archaeological and stylistic classification. Some are so small and shallow that even experienced archaeologists have trouble finding them, while others are so large and deep that we can easily map them from aerial photographs. From berm to berm, ball courts measure from 60 to 250 feet long and from 30 to 90 feet wide. Their builders dug as deep as 9 feet into the earth. We find ball courts almost always at large sites, most often the biggest site in the local community. Some particularly sizable villages had two ball courts, one small and one large. Most ball courts had room for several hundred spectators, and the largest could have held more than 700 people.

Interestingly, the courts are oriented in all directions. David Wilcox suggests that each orientation might be related to an astronomical or mythological event. Together the varied orientations of the ball courts might have represented the set of events in an annual ritual cycle, with participants moving from court to court throughout the year.

The Hohokam began to construct ball courts during the late Pioneer or the early Colonial period,

around 700 CE, although the great majority were built after 900 CE. Most fell out of use between 1050 and 1100; only a few small courts in the Phoenix Basin and the Verde River valley continued to be used after that time. These remaining ball courts might have had local importance, but they clearly lacked the same significance as earlier courts. The demise of the regional ball court network, which I date between about 1050 and 1100, and of the social, religious, and economic systems that supported it, took place at the same time at which we see a dramatic decrease in Hohokam influence and trade goods outside the Phoenix Basin. These events were almost certainly related and mark a significant change in Hohokam culture and history.

How do we know that these structures were ball courts? Early archaeologists believed that the oval depressions were reservoirs, a likely hypothesis given the desert setting of most ball courts. Subsequent excavations, however, revealed that they lacked the silts and other water-deposited sediments one would expect in a reservoir. Instead, they had smoothed and sometimes plastered floors, stone markers, and occasionally defined entry or exit boxes. They resembled similar structures in Mesoamerica in which sixteenth-century Spanish conquistadors had seen ball games played.

Corroborating the Spanish accounts are prehistoric terracotta figurines of ballplayers that indicate that the ball game goes back to at least 1200 BCE in central Mexico (plate 11). People continue to play it today in various forms throughout Mexico and Central America. The Mayas and later the Aztecs played the most famous version of the game. It involved two teams, each vying to knock a heavy rubber ball through a stone ring set several meters above the ground without using their hands or feet. Players hit the ball with their shoulders, hips, and buttocks. They scored points by forcing an opponent to foul and touch the ball with his hands or feet or by knocking the ball through the stone ring or past an end marker. Both commoners and nobles played the game—the nobles sometimes employed professional players—and wagering on the outcome was a favorite pastime for people of all social classes and ranks. The stakes could be high; Spanish accounts say that the losing team was sometimes put to death. We can gauge the importance of this game by accounts from people living on the Gulf Coast of Mexico who paid their annual tribute to Aztec rulers by sending them 16,000 rubber balls. What happened to all those balls remains a mystery. Archaeologists have recovered fewer than 100 in Mesoamerica, and we know of only 3 in the US Southwest.

The Hohokam probably played a ball game most similar to the version that was played in west Mexico at the time of Spanish contact and is still played there today (for more on the Hohokam's connection with Mesoamerica, see chapter 7). Piman speakers in southern Arizona, the likely descendants of the Hohokam, played a variation of it as well during historic times. These games took place on well-defined, cleared, leveled playing fields, although not in courts with stone rings, and often involved heavy gambling and competition between villages. Ritual was an important part of the activities. Several days and nights of feasting, dancing, and other religious undertakings usually preceded the games.

Platform Mounds

Archaeologists define a platform mound as any structure deliberately raised or filled to form an elevated platform. The early Colonial period Hohokam built small, low platform mounds, commonly called "dance mounds," at a few very large sites, such as Snaketown and Gatlin. For example, Mound 16 at Snaketown was approximately 45 feet in diameter and 3 feet high, containing around 7,000 cubic feet of fill. About 1200 CE, Hohokam groups in the Phoenix Basin began to construct larger, more ornate platform mounds that stood taller than a person and contained thousands of cubic feet of fill. Between 1250 and 1350, mound building spread to all major outlying Hohokam regions. Archaeologists have now recorded some 120 platform mounds at more than 95 sites (see map 4). We find mounds, however, in a significantly smaller area than we do ball courts. They appear within the 17,500-square-mile region ranging from the Tucson Basin on the south to the Tonto Basin on the north. The largest mounds stood in the Phoenix Basin, particularly along the Salt River, where the average mound is more than three times the size of those found elsewhere.

Platform mounds vary even more widely in size and construction than do ball courts. They contain anywhere from 2,800 to 500,000 cubic feet of fill, stand between 2 and 12 feet high, and have anywhere from 1 to 30 rooms on top. Hohokam people built each mound inside an adobe-walled compound that usually contained additional ground-floor rooms (fig. 6.4). Many platform mound compounds also have internal walls and possibly guard houses that appear to have restricted access to the mound itself. This limited access indicates that only certain members of the population could enter the interior spaces of the compound, although participants in ceremonies might have used the mound top as a stage visible to outsiders. In contrast, the earlier ball courts were large, open structures probably accessible to all group members. This striking reversal in the structure of ritual architecture suggests the possibility that Hohokam society had become increasingly differentiated and unequal by about 1200, when the large mounds were first constructed.

The function of Hohokam platform mounds has been the subject of debate for more than a hundred

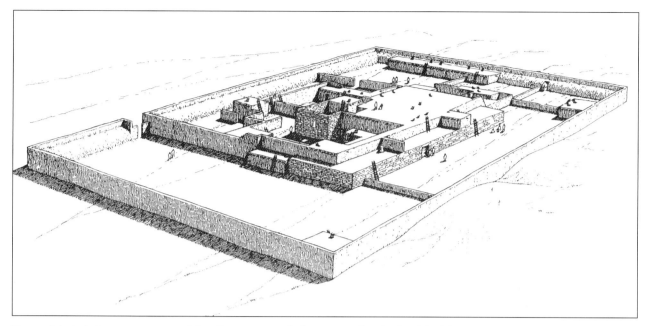

Figure 6.4. Artist's reconstruction of the Cline Terrace platform mound and related buildings within its compound wall.

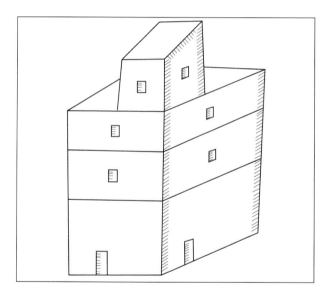

Figure 6.5. A Spanish soldier's sketch of the "Big House" at Casa Grande as first seen in the late 1600s.

years, starting with arguments between Adolph Bandelier and Frank Hamilton Cushing over the Pueblo Grande platform mound in the Phoenix Basin. The debate centers on whether the structures on the mound tops were residential and inhabited by village elites or ceremonial and used only by priests and religious specialists during ritual performances. Archaeologists have tested or excavated more than 20 Hohokam platform mounds.

Although we are still divided over their purpose, all researchers agree that the Hohokam used the mounds to conduct rituals. They constructed the mounds to be seen, and many of them have both a restricted "backstage" area, presumably for preparations for ceremonies, and a public stage in front. Activities on the mound tops would easily have been visible to many hundreds, if not thousands, of people. The mounds might have also been centers for trade, irrigation control, the giving out of food and other goods by leaders, and the integration of outsiders, such as migrant settlers, into the larger social or community group. The wide variation in mound size, construction, and architectural layout suggests that the mounds had many functions.

The Spaniards who arrived in the Southwest in the seventeenth century never saw platform mounds in use, for they had all been long abandoned by that time (fig. 6.5). Ethnographic and ethnohistoric accounts from the southeastern United States and elsewhere, however, suggest that mounds in other regions had both residential and ceremonial functions and their functions often changed over time. Highly visible symbols, they served as both territorial markers and ostentatious displays of individual or group wealth and power.

Figure 6.6. Artist's reconstruction of the Meddler Point platform mound in the Tonto Basin.

The larger the mound, the higher the status of the person or group responsible for its construction, because only very highly ranked elites could command and feed the laborers needed to build such structures.

The Importance of Ritual Architecture

The construction of a ball court or a platform mound offers important information about the nature and complexity of Hohokam social organization. To build either one required substantial group labor under the control of a chief or headman. The archaeologist Douglas Craig, using ethnographic data from Mexico, has estimated that construction of the largest ball courts, such as those found at Snaketown and the Grewe site, demanded 1,000 person-days of labor. To build the platform mound and compound at Meddler Point, a medium-size mound in the Tonto Basin (fig. 6.6), would have required 3,800 person-days. No fewer than 50,000 person-days each would have been necessary to construct the mounds and mound compounds at Pueblo Grande (plate 9) and Mesa Grande (plate 12), the two largest Hohokam platform mounds, both situated on the Salt River arm of the Phoenix Basin.

Of course, the Hohokam did not build these structures quickly. The large mounds undoubtedly took many people many years to build. Such sustained commitment strongly suggests that by the time the Hohokam began to build platform mounds, their society featured highly ranked per-

sons who inherited territories, could command the labor of commoners, and had the foresight required for long-term planning. Indeed, the labor needed to build the large Hohokam mounds rivals that needed to construct some of the large temple mounds in Hawai'i, where nobles had the divinely sanctioned power of life and death over the lower classes. Perhaps Phoenix Basin leaders had similar powers, allowing them to conscript laborers to build their mounds.

In evaluating the function of ball courts and platform mounds, archaeologists identify two primary differences between them. Ball courts were dug down into the earth and were open and accessible to all or most people (fig. 6.7), whereas platform mounds rose up into the sky and were restricted in access. The traditional origin stories of many cultures tell of the people's emergence from below the earth, so subterranean structures might refer to this common beginning. Reaching up into the sky more often relates to elevated status for an individual or group. We cannot be sure whether such symbolism figured in the shift in Hohokam ritual architecture from ball courts to mounds, but many lines of evidence point to a corresponding shift from a more egalitarian society to one with ranked social groups. We know that residents of villages with ball courts often later built platform mounds, but debate continues over whether a few very large sites had both ball courts and platform mounds in use at the same time. Both features served as public stages for rituals important for

Figure 6.7. Onlookers at a dedication ceremony in the Snaketown ball court in the 1960s show how this architectural form accommodated public participation.

maintaining Hohokam society and passing its ideology on to future generations. During these ceremonies, parents likely taught their children to revere the sacredness of place, respect the ancestors, and be one of the people, just as they themselves had learned sitting at their parents' sides.

Even after 100 years of research, archaeologists continue to argue over the nature and function of ball courts and platform mounds, and it is likely that this argument will continue for another century. The fact that the use of these two types of ritual architecture peaked at different times—the pinnacle of ball court use ending around a hundred years prior to true platform mound construction—suggests that they served similar purposes in Hohokam society. Explaining why the Hohokam adopted each of these two architectural forms and eventually ceased to use them is an important arena of current research.

Mark D. Elson is a principal investigator with Desert Archaeology, Inc., and has conducted and published on field research in virtually all Hohokam subareas. At the time of this writing, he was pursuing cross-cultural studies of vulcanism in the archaeological record, sponsored by the National Science Foundation.

Figure 7.1. A Hohokam version of a Mesoamerican mythical creature painted on a Preclassic period bowl from the Tucson Basin.

The Hohokam and Mesoamerica

Randall H. McGuire and Elisa Villalpando C.

The archaeologist Erik Reed once said that he wished the Gadsden Purchase had never happened and the Hohokam had stayed in Mexico where they belonged. Like many other archaeologists who worked in the northern Southwest, Reed found most aspects of Hohokam culture, including architecture, aesthetics, village plans, and iconography, radically different from those of the Ancestral Pueblo peoples he studied. Archaeologists looked to the south, to Mesoamerica, to find the origins of the eccentricity they saw in Hohokam culture. Looking from the north to the south, they asked: How did Mesoamerican culture cross the great unknown sea of northwest Mexico to land on a Hohokam island in southern Arizona? Hohokam migration from the south seemed the obvious answer.

The supposed peculiarities of the Hohokam look much different when the view is from the south to the north. We have worked for more than 25 years in the "great unknown sea of northwest Mexico." Looking from south to north, the Hohokam were not eccentric at all. Rather, they represented the northernmost extension of ways of life, beliefs, and aesthetics that were common to the peoples living along the coast of what is today western Mexico, as far south as the state of Michoacán. What relationship existed between the Hohokam and these southern peoples, and how can we account for the similarities and differences between them?

The Southwest-Northwest and Mesoamerica

In the early part of the twentieth century, anthropologists divided North American Indian peoples into culture areas. One of these culture areas included the Pueblo peoples of the southwestern United States and stretched south into northwestern Mexico to include the indigenous peoples there who made pottery, grew corn, beans, and squash, and dwelled year-round in villages. These "Southwest-Northwest" peoples lived in villages and towns of no more than a few thousand residents, and their largest constructions were Pueblo-like apartment buildings. They had no written languages, social classes, or state-level governments. In terms of the scale of their society, the Hohokam clearly belonged in the Southwest-Northwest culture area.

Figure 7.2. The Hohokam never worked metal but obtained prized copper bells from western Mexico during both the Preclassic and Classic periods.

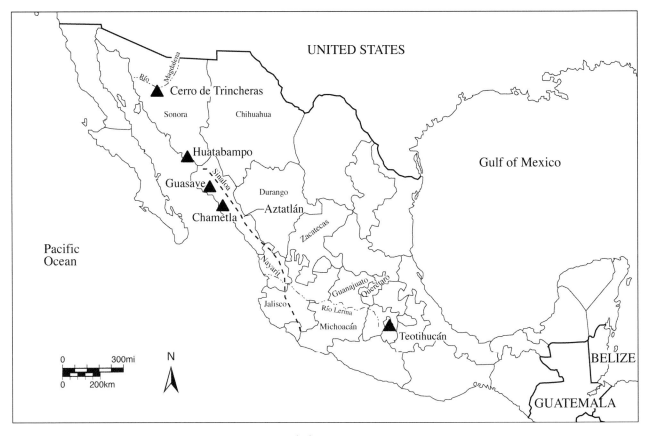

Figure 7.3. Locations in western Mexico important to Hohokam interactions.

To the south, early-twentieth-century anthropologists defined the Mesoamerican culture area, encompassing central Mexico and Guatemala. There, great civilizations, including those of the Olmecs, Aztecs, and Mayas, had flourished. Tribute-taking states ruled these peoples from great cities with tens of thousands of residents and massive pyramids. Many of them developed writing systems and used complex calendars. They shared many aspects of cosmology, a pantheon of gods, and accompanying iconography.

Despite the differences in scale between the Southwest-Northwest and Mesoamerican culture areas, they shared many features, such as serpent deities, masked dancers, and cosmological concepts of directionality, the ritual importance of the cardinal directions, and dualism, a balance between opposing yet complementary entities. The archaeologist Ben Nelson has compared the Southwest-Northwest and Mesoamerica to two languages that share many similar words but have very different grammars. The Hohokam stand out for the number of "words" they shared with the culture area to the south. Indeed, language is more than just a metaphor. The majority of languages spoken in both culture areas belong to the Uto-Aztecan family, and the Hohokam likely spoke a language or languages in this family. Many of the similarities between the two culture areas probably originated with the spread of this language family and maize agriculture.

Another reason to view the Hohokam as a people sharing characteristics of both culture areas is that the boundary between the Southwest-Northwest and Mesoamerica is ill defined and changed over time. Mesoamerican cultures spread north of the Río Lerma, between Michoacán and Jalisco, in the last few centuries before the common era (fig. 7.3). They reached their northernmost extent in the Mexican state of Durango by 1200 CE and then receded southward. Along the west coast of Mexico, from Sinaloa in the north to Michoacán in the south, a distinctive West Mexican subregion of Mesoamerica developed in conjunction with Mesoamerican expansion. By 900 CE, this West Mexican culture extended northward to the boundary between the contemporary states of Sonora and Sinaloa, reaching a maximum proximity to the Hohokam.

Archaeologists have done more research in Mesoamerica and the southwestern United States than in virtually any other part of the Americas. But the region from the present-day US-Mexico border south to the Río Lerma has been one of the least researched regions of North America. US archaeologists have been hesitant to cross the border, and Mexican archaeologists have tended to focus their research on the great cities and pyramids of Mesoamerica. Without a clear understanding of northern Mexico, archaeologists have often treated Mesoamerica as a uniform cultural area from which the Hohokam could have drawn cultural traits like picking beans from a sack. For example, Emil Haury suggested that the Hohokam began as a Mesoamerican society in search of a new home. Moving north, they carried few material goods with them and left no trace along the route, but they were heavily laden with a Mesoamerican culture. They moved quickly across an arid northern Mexico until they found their promised land in the Phoenix Basin. There they unpacked their Mesoamerican heritage of aesthetics, architecture, and artifacts.

In the past 25 years, archaeologists working in southern Arizona and in Mexico have discredited this immigrants' tale. In southern Arizona, archaeologists have demonstrated that agriculture, irrigation, ceramics, and village life did not enter the region from outside as a package. Rather, they developed in place over hundreds of years. We also know now that Mesoamerica is a complex region with great internal variation and fuzzy boundaries. Our own research in Sonora, Mexico, is part of a recent movement of US, Canadian, and Mexican researchers that has shed light on the poorly known cultural traditions of northwestern and western Mexico. In this context of new knowledge, we would agree with Erik Reed that the Hohokam before the Classic period belonged to the Mexican sphere.

What Is Mesoamerican about the Hohokam?
Many aspects of Hohokam aesthetics, architecture, and artifacts reflect Mesoamerican origins, suggesting that the Hohokam also shared some elements of Mesoamerican cosmology, customs, and social organization. But the similarities do not link the Hohokam directly with the well-known core civilizations of Mesoamerica, such as the Olmec, Maya, and Aztec. Instead, they spring from West Mexican cultures.

Mesoamerican influence appears throughout the Hohokam sequence. Early Hohokam artifact styles included simple bowls with four-part, bilaterally symmetrical designs (fig. 7.4) and pinched-face figurines—styles also found in Mesoamerica. The Pioneer period Hohokam lived in pithouses arranged in courtyard groups and practiced cremation, as did some peoples of northern and central Mexico. Mesoamerican influence intensified toward the end of the Pioneer period, reaching its height during the later Colonial and Sedentary periods, between about 700 and 1100 CE. In the Classic period, Hohokam culture most closely resembled the Salado and other late prehistoric cultural developments of the US Southwest, but we also find a few items typical of Mesoamerica, such as *comales* (tortilla grills), molded spindle whorls, and drop-ended manos (handheld grinding stones with downturned ends that fit over narrow metates, or lower grinding stones).

Hohokam aesthetics differed markedly from those of ancient peoples in other parts of the southwestern United States. The Hohokam's widespread use of anthropomorphic (human-like) and zoomorphic (animal-like) figures on ceramics and shell jewelry is one artistic style that distinguishes them from their northern neighbors. Hohokam symbols associated with rituals and beliefs most clearly show a Mesoamerican connection. Some motifs, such as representations of serpents, are so widely distributed in North America that they probably had no single point of origin. But other images clearly link the Hohokam to Mesoamerica. The depiction of a bird eating a snake appears throughout Mesoamerica and survives to this day on the flag of Mexico. The Hohokam carved this image on shell jewelry (fig. 7.5) along with intertwined serpents and snakes swallowing snakes, which also echo common Mesoamerican motifs. The same is true of the frogs, coyotes, birds, and mythical animals that the Hohokam

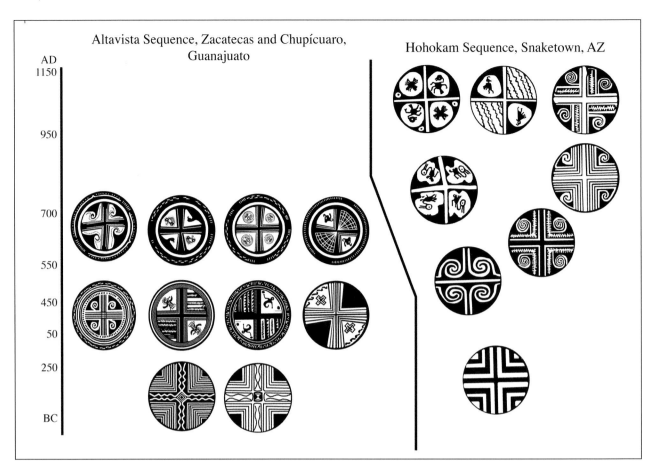

Altavista Sequence, Zacatecas and Chupícuaro, Guanajuato

Hohokam Sequence, Snaketown, AZ

AD
1150

950

700

550

450

50

250

BC

Figure 7.4. Comparison of four-part, bilaterally symmetrical designs on Hohokam and West Mexican bowls from the sites of Alta Vista in Zacatecas and Chupícuaro in Guanajuato.

executed on ceramics and in carved shell (fig. 7.1).

Both the layout and form of Hohokam architecture also resembled Mesoamerican styles. As Craig and Henderson describe in chapter 4, Hohokam households lived in courtyard groups consisting of two or more pithouses facing a common courtyard, with work areas and trash dumps around the periphery. In the Classic period these courtyard groups developed into walled residential compounds. Throughout Mesoamerica, archaeologists find similar household plans, which they call patio groups. Patio groups, too, developed through time into walled residential compounds.

The ball court is one of the best pieces of evidence linking the Hohokam and Mesoamerica. Archaeologists have identified more than 225 of these courts on Hohokam sites. The ball game played in similar courts was one of the defining characteristics of Mesoamerica, and a few indige-

Figure 7.5. A carved shell ring from the Grewe site displays the common Hohokam motif of a bird eating a snake. See the similar motif in figure 3.8.

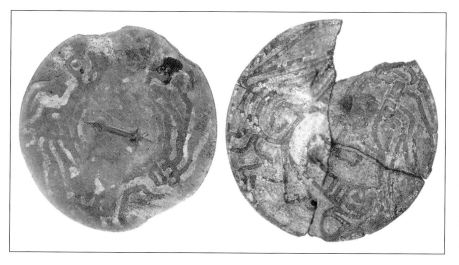

Figure 7.6. The sandstone backs of these iron pyrite mirrors from the Grewe site are decorated in pseudo-cloisonné with designs of Mesoamerican style.

nous groups still play it today (plate 11, and see chapter 6). The elite form of the game used a long, narrow, T- or I-shaped court with straight walls and two stone rings mounted one on each wall. A team could win the game by putting a solid rubber ball about the size of a volleyball through one of the stone rings. In the plazas of towns and villages, commoners played a version of the game that required a team to pass and return the ball without allowing it to hit the ground. In both games, players could not touch the ball with their hands. Archaeologists dispute whether the Hohokam used their courts to play a version of the ball game or, alternatively, as dance plazas. The discovery at some Hohokam sites of prehistoric balls made from the rubbery sap of a desert shrub suggests that the Hohokam played the ball game. If they did play the Mesoamerican game, then they played the commoners' version. Teams could not have played the elite form of the game in Hohokam ball courts because they lacked the straight sides and stone rings necessary for that contest.

Artifacts, too, speak of the connections between Mesoamerican and Hohokam peoples. Archaeolo-gists have occasionally found objects at Hohokam sites that came directly from Mesoamerica. Far more common are items that were produced locally but display forms and decorative techniques that scholars believe originated in Mesoamerica.

Probably all the Mesoamerican objects in

Hohokam sites came from West Mexico. They in-clude several hundred copper bells, some iron pyrite mirrors, and fragments from a few pottery vessels. The backs of the mirrors were made of sandstone and decorated using a West Mexican technique known as pseudo-cloisonné (fig. 7.6). A craftsperson covered the stone with layers of colored pigment and then carved through the layers to expose the different hues. The Huichol Indians of the Mexican state of Jalisco still use a similar technique to decorate gourds for sale to tourists. We think that these mirrors are West Mexican versions of the pyrite and obsidian mirrors found in central Mesoamerican cities and that shamans used them to divine the future. In addition to artifacts, zooarchaeologists have identified among the animal bones from Hohokam sites the remains of macaws from the tropical lowlands of West Mexico. All these rare and exotic items were likely elite status goods.

Mesoamerican stylistic influences appear to have reached the Hohokam from western Mexico as well. Archaeologists see these influences most prevalently in ceramic figurines and in shell jewelry, one of the most distinctive aspects of Hohokam art. Artisans obtained the shells for their work from the coast of the Gulf of California. Most often they made bracelets made out of *Glycymeris* and *Lavicardium* shells, two types of bivalves. They also crafted shell tinklers, pendants, rings, and beads. In the finest examples, artisans carved and etched motifs on the shell. The Hohokam made many male and female ceramic figurines simply by folding together two rods of clay and then pinching, incising, and applying bits of clay to depict bodily features, tattooing or body painting, clothing, headdresses, and jewelry. Less commonly, they produced hollow, doll-like forms or ceramic vessels in human form. Both the elaborate figurine complex itself and certain aspects of the body decoration and clothing portrayed on the figurines reflect distinctively West Mexican styles.

Northern Mexico

All this evidence of a western Mexican influence on the Hohokam tells us that they were not an eccentric, unique, and isolated people. What looks like an island of Mesoamerican influence when viewed from the north becomes the tip of a peninsula when examined from the south.

In West Mexico, early village life, pottery making, and agricultural traditions began a few hundred years before the common era. These early beginnings look much like the Pioneer period Hohokam. In southern Sinaloa, archaeologists call the first such tradition, dating from 250 BCE to 500 CE, Chametla Temprano. There, the earliest pottery has crude, broad-lined red designs laid out in quarters, bilaterally symmetrical, over a cream-colored slip. By the 600s these traditions had begun to look very Mesoamerican. For example, people built towns with planned mound-and-plaza complexes oriented to the cardinal directions. Elaborate figurine styles, molded spindle whorls, red-on-brown or red-on-buff pottery, and shell jewelry (mostly bracelets) also appear in the West Mexican archaeological record about this time. A distinctive development in these traditions was copper metallurgy, which artisans most commonly used to produce bells. Do these artifacts sound familiar? Archaeologists find very similar items in Hohokam sites.

In central Mexico, the Mesoamerican core, the collapse of the great city of Teotihuacán by 900 CE brought about great changes, including the flourishing of new cultural traditions and the expansion of Mesoamerican cultures to the north and west. In West Mexico a new tradition that archaeologists call the Aztatlán Complex developed. It included copper metallurgy, the use of prismatic obsidian blades (fashioned into a long, narrow shape using a Mesoamerican technique), pseudo-cloisonné decoration, ceramic pipes, very elaborate figurines and effigy vessels, and spindle whorls. The most distinctive aspect of the Aztatlán Complex was ceramics decorated in a Mixteca-Puebla style that appears throughout Mesoamerica. This complex stretched from Michoacán to Sinaloa and lasted until 1400. The imported Mesoamerican items that we find among the Hohokam originated in this tradition and its immediate predecessors.

The Sonoran Desert Traditions

In addition to Mesoamerican connections of a general nature, recent research concentrated in Sonora has demonstrated links between the Hohokam and a series of peoples living in West Mexico. The Huatabampo tradition straddled the modern border between Sonora and Sinaloa. Its distinctive styles first appeared in the archaeological record by about 200 BCE and about 700 years later merged with the Gusave and Aztatlán Complexes to the south. Huatabampo people made figurines that are stylistically similar to those of the Hohokam, and they also made and used drop-ended manos. We now think that these manos were a Sonoran Desert phenomenon and not a Mesoamerican import.

In northern Sonora, the Magdalena River runs to the sea and helped to support the people of the Trincheras tradition, who appear in the archaeological record in the first centuries of the common era and thrived until after 1400. The earliest pottery in the region is very much like that of southern Arizona in the same period. By 200 CE, a distinctive Trincheras ceramic tradition of reddish pottery decorated with purple paint emerged. Like the Hohokam, the Trincheras people practiced cremation and built pithouses in patio (courtyard) groups. They also constructed villages on terraced hills (the *cerros de trincheras* for which they are named), an architectural form that found its way to the Hohokam by the Classic period. Like their Huatabampo and Hohokam neighbors, Trincheras people used drop-ended manos.

A final item linking the Hohokam to these Sonoran and West Mexico cultures is the production of shell jewelry. The Hohokam made their shell jewelry from the same species that their southern neighbors did, decorated it in similar ways, and made mostly bracelets. Their artistic output represents the northernmost extent of a shell jewelry tradition that extended from West Mexico to the Hohokam area and transcended the boundary between the Southwest-Northwest and Mesoamerica. Both the Huatabampo and Trincheras

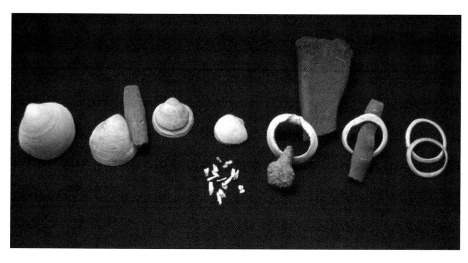

Figure 7.7. Bracelet makers from western Mexico to southern Arizona cut rings from whole shells, then polished the sharp edges with granular stone implements.

people made abundant shell jewelry. Along the western coastal plain from Nayarit inland to southern Arizona, we find shell bracelets that are stylistically indistinguishable (fig. 7.7). Hohokam artisans introduced the use of acid etching, and Trincheras craftspeople were especially fond of sea turtle motifs, but aside from such regional differences, our impression is of striking similarities.

Changing Influences

The uniqueness of the Hohokam as an island of Mesoamerican-influenced culture in the US Southwest is an illusion of perspective and lack of information. Looking from north to south, the Hohokam before the Classic period appear strikingly different from the cultures of the Pueblo Southwest. Archaeological research since the late 1980s has allowed us to take a different perspective, looking from Mesoamerica northward. From this viewpoint, the Hohokam emerge as the northernmost and latest of a long series of related developments. The pithouses, four-part pottery designs, and figurines of the Hohokam Pioneer period greatly resemble slightly earlier developments in western Mexico. By the 500s CE, the Hohokam were participants in a chain of interactions that stretched into West Mexico and involved the trading of elite goods such as copper bells, iron pyrite mirrors, and macaws and the borrowing of art

styles and architecture. As the cultures of West Mexico became more Mesoamerican in character, we see more Mesoamerican items and styles among the Hohokam.

During the Hohokam Classic period, the peoples of southern Arizona became more strongly linked east to west as part of the Salado phenomenon, a new stylistic tradition marked by polychrome pottery—that is, pottery decorated in three or more colors—that originated to the east and became widespread across the region. The Hohokam shifted their preferences in elite goods from West Mexican forms to the polychrome pottery and turquoise-on-shell mosaics characteristic of the broader US Southwest. At this point the Hohokam stand out less because the later Mesoamerican influences, particularly the Mesoamerican-inspired motifs on Salado polychrome pottery, are relatively common throughout the Southwest. The Hohokam had once belonged to the Mexican sphere; now they were part of the great Southwest.

Randall H. McGuire is a professor of anthropology at New York State University, Binghamton. His principal interests lie in the development of power relations in the past, historical archaeology, social theory, and archaeomagnetic dating. He has worked extensively in the US Southwest and northwestern Mexico, including a long-term project at Cerro de Trincheras. Elisa Villalpando is an *investigadora* with the Instituto Nacional de Antropología e Historia, Centro INAH Sonora. Her wide-ranging interests in northern Mexico include ethnohistory, the transition to agriculture, cultural resource management, shell analysis, and Seri archaeology and ethnology. She co-directs research at the Early Agricultural period site of La Playa and at Cerro de Trincheras.

Figure 8.1. Preclassic Hohokam pottery came alive with painted people, birds, snakes, turtles, mammals, and other life forms, often repeated across the surfaces of vessels.

Hohokam Ceramics, Hohokam Beliefs

Stephanie M. Whittlesey

Rounded, smooth, cool to the touch—a ceramic container is much more than an infinitely useful piece of household equipment. It can be decorative, a canvas for artistic expression, and a signal of the time when it was created. Ceramics can symbolize deeply held beliefs and serve as a medium in which people express their identity. For these reasons, ceramic containers are a rich source of information for archaeologists, and the Hohokam ceramic tradition is no exception. We have learned much that we know about the Hohokam through their ceramics. Many years ago, archaeologists used the distinctive red-on-buff pottery, so unlike the black-on-white, red-on-brown, and polychrome wares made by other ancient peoples in the Southwest, to identify the Hohokam culture and map its boundaries. Ceramics and their stratigraphic order also defined the Hohokam cultural sequence through time. Today, archaeologists can match the chemistry of the clay and the minerals in it to their natural sources, allowing us to determine where containers were made and how they were distributed. A pot is not simply a pot, but a visual and tactile record of past human lives and behaviors.

In this chapter I use ceramics to explore Hohokam ideology, beliefs, and ritual. To do so, I delve into the sources of Hohokam culture, connections between the Hohokam and prehistoric Mexican peoples, and the unusual character of the pottery itself. Many archaeologists believe that the Hohokam were a peripheral Mesoamerican people who immigrated to their Arizona home, perhaps from somewhere in western coastal Mexico (but see chapters 2 and 7 for alternative views). Evidence supporting

this belief lies in many aspects of Hohokam lifeways and artifacts, including ceramics. In materials, forms, and designs, Hohokam pottery is unlike anything else made in the US Southwest, but it shares features with pottery found in what is today western Mexico. If we are correct in assuming an intimate link between the Hohokam and Mesoamerican cultures, then we can extrapolate the idea that the two cultures shared belief systems, iconography, and sacred architecture (see chapter 6).

What is pottery, exactly? Some readers may understand *ceramics* to mean high-fired wares, such as porcelain, and *pottery* to mean low-fired earthenware, but archaeologists use the terms interchangeably to mean the latter when discussing the prehistoric cultures of the US Southwest. Regardless of their label, ceramics represent a unique composite of earth, water, and fire—elements transformed by being fired into a glasslike material.

To set the stage for my exploration of meaning and symbol, I need to outline the way Hohokam people made pottery. I look only at ceramics made before about 1150 CE, the time archaeologists call the Preclassic period. Hohokam lifeways, including pottery making, changed so dramatically and in so many ways during the subsequent Classic period that I prefer to restrict the frame of reference. I also discuss only ceramics made in the so-called core area where the Hohokam culture was first defined—the Phoenix Basin along the Gila and Salt Rivers. Outside this area, Hohokam pottery was variable, and that is a topic worthy of another essay.

I use the generic term *potter* because we do not know whether Hohokam potters were men or

Figure 8.2. An Akimel O'odham potter in the early 1900s forms clay coils to initially shape a pot.

Figure 8.3. The potter flattens the coils by paddling them against an anvil held inside the vessel.

women (see also chapter 3). Across the world and over the centuries, women have made the utilitarian containers they used in everyday life. There are some hints that Hohokam ceramic production was more complicated than this, a topic I return to later. For now, the gender of the ancient potters remains a mystery.

The Preclassic Hohokam created two common kinds of pottery from two different pastes, or prepared clays. They made plain ware—pottery without any kind of decoration—from a coarse paste that looked brownish gray after firing. This type of clay is called a primary or residual clay—one that has weathered in place from its parent material. The paste used to make pottery must contain temper, or tiny particles of a hard material, for strength and to

Figure 8.4. Using a rounded pebble, the potter smoothes the surface of the fully shaped jar prior to firing.

avoid cracking during firing. Temper can be any nonclay material, and Hohokam potters used crushed micaceous schist, a kind of metamorphic rock, for this purpose. The silver mica in the schist particles gave the plain ware vessels a sparkle, as if they had been dipped in glitter.

When they planned to decorate their containers, potters used a different and much finer paste. This one fired to a buff color and contained only a small quantity of crushed schist, in order not to obscure the painted design. There is no obvious functional or technical reason for mixing schist rather than some other temper into the paste. I believe that it had a deeper significance, which I discuss later.

Archaeologists have squabbled over the sources of these raw materials. The brown-firing clay used in plain ware can be found over much of southern Arizona, so there is little mystery to it. But we are still unsure where potters collected the buff-firing clay, or even whether the material was entirely natural. The buff clay is a sedimentary, or secondary, clay—one that has been weathered from a source and then transported by wind or water to the deposit where it is found. Sedimentary clays are extremely scarce in central and southern Arizona,

and no one has ever located an exact source for the buff clay. Some archaeologists have speculated that the Hohokam dug settling basins or reservoirs to collect buff clay, which settled out from the water. They might have gathered clay from canals in the same way. The source of the schist temper, too, is ambiguous. The emerging consensus is that Hohokam potters collected schist from only a few sources in the Phoenix Basin, particularly at a landform called Gila Butte. Hohokam artisans also used this gray, subtly shining stone to fashion palettes used in ritual performances.

Like all potters of the prehistoric Southwest, Hohokam potters worked without benefit of wheel or mold. They shaped the clay, temper, and water mixture into the chosen form with their own hands. Beginning with a flat slab base, the potter stacked fat coil upon fat coil (fig. 8.2) and bonded the coils together with a paddle and anvil (fig. 8.3), literally beating the clay into shape. When satisfied with the shape, the potter smoothed the surface by hand and lightly polished it with a stone (fig. 8.4).

Painting was the next step, if the pot was decorated. Artisans—again, we cannot say whether the potter who made the container also decorated it, or

Figure 8.5. Like their Hohokam predecessors, O'odham potters fired their pots outdoors rather than in kilns.

cause pieces to pop off the surface or make the pot explode. The temperature must be just right, and painted pots must be covered with old, broken pots to keep soot from blackening the designs. I have watched modern potters perform little rituals before firing to ensure that their pots survive intact. No doubt Hohokam potters did the same.

How did the Hohokam use these vessels? They designed most pots with function in mind. Storage containers had fat, round bodies and short, constricted necks that could be covered with mud, leather, or ceramic lids to protect their contents. A pot stores corn and other foodstuffs

whether the artists were men or women—painted red designs with a hematite, or iron oxide, mixture. The painters were skilled artists who depicted human dancers linking arms, flocks of birds in flight, snakes with curling tails, and hordes of tiny tortoises or turtles that seem to leap into life. Some potters painted geometric patterns that seem to swirl across the vessel surface like "op art" from the 1960s. Other, more staid designs stack parallel lines together to form four-part patterns (see fig. 7.3). The Hohokam did not make the black-on-white ware that is the hallmark of Ancestral Pueblo culture.

The potter then set the pot aside to dry slowly —again, we do not know exactly how. In the hot Arizona sun, rapid drying would have been risky, potentially causing cracks to form in the pot. The potter might have set the green pot in a relatively cool, dry place indoors or covered it with damp cloth or grass. When the pots were completely dry, potters fired them in the open, using a wood fire and little else (fig. 8.5). The Hohokam did not build kilns, as far as we can determine.

Firing is the most troublesome step in the entire pot-making process. If the pot is insufficiently dry, it will crack. Any bit of stray material or certain kinds of rock included in the clay by accident might

much more securely than a container made of basketry. Most storage containers were plain ware, although painted containers may have been used to store water and other liquids. Oddly, cooking vessels—identified by their shape and the wear left from use—are scarce in Hohokam sites. Hohokam cuisine was based on meal made from ground seeds and maize kernels, and we think that large pieces of broken vessels, even painted ones, were used to parch seeds and toast tortilla-like breads.

Painted pottery served ritual as well as domestic functions. The Hohokam burned incense and mineral substances in thick-bodied censers, perhaps to create intensely colored flames during ritual performances. Pottery also played an important ceremonial role in funeral rites. The Hohokam cremated their dead, placed the ashes in large vessels, often covered with an upturned bowl, and buried them. Pottery vessels, sometimes deliberately shattered, accompanied the cremated remains. The Hohokam also buried fired-clay figurines of humans and animals, sometimes also smashed and burned, as offerings. They fashioned much of their painted pottery into exotic forms such as tripod vessels, censers, human or animal effigy vessels, and bowls with widely flaring rims (fig. 8.6; plate 5). The impracticality of these forms reinforces archaeologists' belief

Figure 8.6. Hohokam potters produced a diversity of vessel forms, including many that have no apparent everyday use.

that they had ritual purposes. Many of these shapes resemble those of vessels made in prehistoric Mexico (see chapter 7).

With this brief description of the technology and uses of Hohokam pottery, we can now turn to pottery's unseen functions—a realm where the waters are clouded and meaning is unclear. I have forwarded the idea that the Hohokam were an ancient Mesoamerican people. As such, they shared many of the basic cosmological principles, deities, religious rituals, and iconography that made Mesoamerican religion so complicated and mystical. At the heart of this belief system was the notion of bringing rain to water the crops, fill the irrigation canals, and ensure that wild plants grew lush with fruit and seeds. Water was essential to the Hohokam, who built a lifeway dependent on irrigated farming in a land of little natural rainfall.

Informed speculation suggests that a rain cult much like that devoted to the ancient Mesoamerican rain-storm-earth god, Tlaloc, was central to Hohokam religion. The Tlaloc cult was dedicated to bringing rain for crops. Many symbols connected Tlaloc with water—mountains, serpents, marine shells, and ceramic containers. Mountains and volcanoes were powerful and evocative landscape metaphors. The people believed that mountains generated rain, springs, lakes, and streams. Mesoamericans therefore described mountains metaphorically as containers, or vessels, in which water was stored; mountains were impressive symbols for water. In addition to water, the mountain's hollow heart, representing the sacred cave from which all life came, held maize and other treasures.

Because of the mountain's intimate connection to rain, the ancient Mexicans believed that the deity Tlaloc made his home on the mountain. Indeed, the name *Tlaloc* was derived from the Nahuatl word *tlalli*, meaning "earth," and the suffix *oc*, implying "something lying upon the surface." This label referred to the thunderclouds that boil up over mountains in the rainy season. Priests

Figure 8.7. Long-legged water birds attack a snake on a plate from Tucson dating between 750 and 900 CE.

carried out ceremonies and sacrifices to Tlaloc on mountain peaks, particularly at the beginning of the rainy season.

The mountain and cave metaphors carried over into the built environment. To ancient Mesoamerican peoples, the flat-topped, stepped pyramid represented a mountain, and the temple on top symbolized the natural cave. Ceremonial centers contained precincts composed of one or more pyramids, temples, and ball courts, often dedicated to Tlaloc, Quetzalcoatl, and other deities. Priests carried out rituals on the pyramids within the ceremonial precinct.

Serpents symbolized the connection between underworld and upperworld. The people believed that the serpent's mouth was a symbolic cave, and serpents were considered bearers of or conduits for water. Many deities, particularly those connected to rain and water, had a serpent aspect. The best known is Quetzalcoatl, the feathered serpent who brought wind and rain. Images of Tlaloc show him holding lightning serpents and other water symbols. Water deities were also depicted wearing shell jewelry, and the ancient Mexicans offered coral, shells, and other items from the sea to the gods of rain and water.

Figure 8.8. Gila Butte, near Snaketown, furnished shiny mica temper for Preclassic red-on-buff pottery, which was traded throughout the Hohokam world.

Ceramic containers, too, were vital symbols of rain. The myths about Tlaloc tell that he lives in a patio with four jars in each corner. When lightning strikes the jars, water pours forth to fall as rain. Ceramic containers represented caves as well, which were thought to be entrances to the underworld—the home of the ancestors—and powerful sources of water, rain, and springs. Ceramic vessels, caves, mountains, the underground, the ancestors, and water were thus linked metaphorically in a complex way.

How, then, did Hohokam potters express their beliefs, translating water metaphors into the medium of fired clay? The symbolic connection between water and ceramic containers probably was extremely ancient in the Southwest, going all the way back to the Archaic period, a time before people made ceramic containers. Archaic people understood how to take clay, mix it with water, and fire it. They created intriguing fired-clay figurines from a fine, light-colored clay like that found in springs and *ciénegas*, or wetlands. Some archaeologists think that they used such figurines as offerings to bring rain and ensure fertility, among other things. The offerings would have been the more powerful because they were made of clay taken from a water source.

Pots themselves were symbols of water, as we

have seen, and vessels were made from materials carrying water symbolism. Water symbolism is everywhere in the painted decoration of Hohokam pots. Water birds, fish, snakes, turtles, and squirmy, tadpole-like shapes—all creatures that live in or near the water and that symbolized water to ancient Mesoamericans—glide across the painted containers (fig. 8.7). The Hohokam repeated these symbols of water in other media, such as stone and shell carvings. Even their geometric designs spoke of water—scrolls resembling curling waves or serpents, feathered scrolls that could evoke Quetzalcoatl, and terraced motifs representing clouds.

The glittering surface of plain ware has been likened to the sparkle of sun on water, although it might also have symbolized stars or other phenomena. The Hohokam mined the schist that created this glittering surface at Gila Butte and possibly a few other places in the Gila River valley. All Hohokam pottery therefore contained bits of what may have been the most sacred landmark in Hohokam cosmology and myth.

Gila Butte is a double-crested peak that stands 500 feet above the Gila River (fig. 8.8). From Interstate 10 heading toward Phoenix, one sees Gila Butte rising to the east, high above the searing plain, just after crossing the Gila River bridge. One imagines climbing to the top and surveying the entire valley—the view stretches for miles. Gila Butte is an outcrop of hard, durable, metamorphic rock that forces the Gila River to curve around its base. A few miles west of Gila Butte lies the site of Snaketown. This important site was an enormous residential and ceremonial center with several early forms of ceremonial platform mounds (see chapter 6) and two ball courts around a large central plaza, nearly 60 trash mounds (long-term, mounded accumulations of residential trash), and hundreds of houses. It was a focal point of the Hohokam world for at least 500 years.

In the arid landscape along the Gila River, Gila Butte must have held a prominent place. Its hard bedrock raised the water table, making it easier to tap the river with canals. The Hohokam living at Snaketown built their main irrigation canal at the foot of Gila Butte. Water, the substance of life, therefore literally flowed from the mountain. The butte is crisscrossed with foot trails, and we find evidence on it of stone quarrying.

Was Gila Butte more than just a good place to construct a canal and to get stone for pottery temper and ritual objects? I think it was. Gila Butte was myth given substance and place, a fusion of the vital and the sacred. It might have been the Hohokam creation story set in stone. I have described the connection between mountains and water in Mesoamerican belief, and mountains figure prominently in the creation stories of Mesoamerican peoples. Coatépec, or Snake Mountain, is an ancient mythical symbol in many such stories. On their long migration from their place of origin, the ancient Mexicans were beset by hunger, thirst, and other trials. They stopped at Snake Mountain to rest and build a temple devoted to the deity Huitzilopochtli on the mountain top. The god answered the people's prayers by creating a ball court at the base of the mountain. It contained a hole, or "skull place," from which water flowed. A lake formed, providing water for cultivation and sustenance, and saved the people.

We can see all the elements of this ancient story replicated at Gila Butte. It was a natural, living pyramid, a mountain symbolizing water. Water flowed from the mountain's base in the form of a major irrigation canal, bringing water to the fields at Snaketown and sustaining the people who lived there. I think that it is no coincidence that the ceremonial center of Snaketown, with its enormous ball court and central plaza surrounded by mounds, was situated near Gila Butte. Throughout Mesoamerica, people often located their large ceremonial centers at natural features such as caves, springs, and cenotes, water-holding sinkholes or depressions. The proximity of such important landscape metaphors gave the ceremonial center power. Mountains and smoking volcanoes were impressive backdrops for their human-built counterparts and for ceremonies taking place on pyramids and in ball courts. Snaketown must have gained tremendous ritual power (and, as we will see, political power) from its proximity to Gila Butte. (I should note that the name *Snaketown* is wholly coincidental. The Akimel O'odham people who lived there

long after the Hohokam abandoned the village named it "The Place of Many Snakes," and Emil Haury and Harold Gladwin, archaeologists who excavated Snaketown, translated the name into English.)

Returning to ceramics, we know that Hohokam potters fashioned their ceramic containers to symbolize water. But we do not understand well the economic context of Hohokam ceramic production. Some scholars believe that craft specialists made pottery in a standardized process. At Snaketown, for example, archaeologists have found evidence for pottery workshops, and nowhere else do we find such a large percentage of painted pottery among all the potsherds collected. Regardless of who made them, pottery vessels were produced in quantity at Snaketown. Each pot contained pieces of the sacred mountain, Gila Butte. We can imagine that rituals performed with such containers were enhanced, prayers said over them were more effective, and the stored food and water the vessels contained were considered blessed. It is possible that certain containers were required for Hohokam rituals or to bury the cremated dead, which would explain the distribution of Hohokam pottery to far-flung settlements across Arizona.

These links among craft and ritual, monuments and meaning, farming and ideology were profound, complex, and deeply ingrained in all aspects of Hohokam life. By combining control of the sacred and the mundane, the Hohokam built a strong and enduring society on water control and facilitated its survival through ideology and ritual. Gila Butte's natural characteristics made irrigation farming there easier. At the same time, Gila Butte was a powerful ideological instrument, a symbol that enhanced farming, encouraged bountiful harvests, and ensured that the river did not fail. The twin-peaked natural pyramid might have inspired the Hohokam to build their great ceremonial center of Snaketown and might have represented the core of Hohokam identity. In this way, the means of production and the supporting ideological framework blended seamlessly.

Hohokam ceramics confirm the statement with which I began—a pot is not just a pot; it is much more. It is worth remembering these connections and embedded meanings when visiting a museum, seeing a ceramic vessel illustrated in a magazine, or driving by Gila Butte. Remember that to many prehistoric people, and certainly to the Hohokam, a ceramic container fused multiple meanings and metaphors into a fluid construction—rounded, smooth, and cool to the touch.

Stephanie M. Whittlesey is principal investigator and senior project manager for SWCA Environmental Consultants. She is well known for her publications on past cultural landscapes in southern Arizona, the role of ideology in shaping ancient life, the analysis of ceramic technology and style, and the history of Southwestern archaeology.

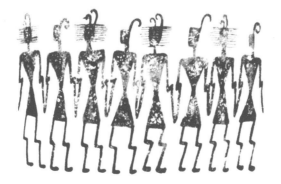

Figure 9.1. Hohokam people of all ages wore bracelets made from marine shells.

Artisans and Their Crafts in Hohokam Society

James M. Bayman

In the desert soils of south-central Arizona, archaeologists unearth polished shell jewelry (fig. 9.1) and pottery painted with bold red designs, in craft styles unique to this part of the ancient Southwest. Harold Gladwin, Emil Haury, and other early-twentieth-century archaeologists found so many ornaments made from marine shells and so many red-on-buff ceramic vessels that they declared them—along with ball courts—the hallmarks of Hohokam culture. As evidence of the importance of crafts like these in Hohokam life, archaeologists find raw materials, by-products of manufacturing, and finished products almost everywhere they excavate, including house floors, storage pits, household garbage accumulations, agricultural fields, hunting stations, and ritual buildings such as platform mounds.

When archaeologists study a "craft tradition," they investigate the materials and technologies used in manufacture, as well as the culture-specific sense of style that guided the crafting process. They are also interested in the social, economic, and political roles of crafts and in how the tradition developed through time. Determining how the Hohokam made, used, and thought about crafts is particularly challenging because their descendants were no longer making the same range of items when Spaniards first wrote down observations about them in the late seventeenth century. For example, post-contact O'odham potters went about making their vessels in the same basic manner as their Hohokam predecessors, but they did not paint their pottery with Hohokam designs and symbols. The O'odham no longer made or traded for objects such as figurines, palettes, censers, shell pendants set with

turquoise, and copper bells that the Hohokam had used in their social, political, and ritual life.

Craft Traditions

The Hohokam made certain kinds of tools and pottery for everyday uses, and they fashioned other goods, especially the kinds we would characterize as artistic or ornamental, as symbols of status or affiliation and for use in rituals. Village artisans made implements such as stone axes (fig. 9.2) to fell trees and shape roof posts, as well as manos and metates to grind corn kernels and other seeds into flour. Hohokam artisans also made knives, scrapers, and arrow points from stone suited for chipping, such as chert and obsidian, in order to hunt game and process the meat and hides. They used other kinds of stone to fashion religious and ceremonial

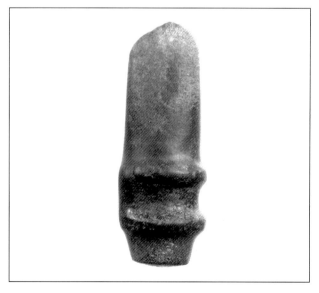

Figure 9.2. Polished stone axe with groove for hafting.

objects. They sought stone that occurred naturally in thin plates to make palettes with flat, even surfaces. Relatively soft, easily carved types of stone served for making bowl-like censers for burning incense, pipes for smoking, human and animal figures, and small stone vessels with carved decorations (fig. 9.3).

Figure 9.3. Hohokam artisans of the Preclassic period carved a variety of small stone vessels, often decorated with human and animal figures.

Sometimes craft items appear to have served both everyday and special social purposes, as on the rare occasions when Hohokam mourners placed several thousand arrow points in a grave as an offering or indication of the deceased person's role in society. Similarly, Hohokam potters routinely fabricated ordinary clay vessels in varied shapes and sizes for cooking, serving, and storing food. Rarely, they also fashioned marvelous effigy pots in the shapes of creatures such as birds and bighorn sheep and of men and women complete with painted renderings of clothing, jewelry, and body paint or tattoos (plates 3 and 4).

The limits of preservation determine what we can know about any ancient craft tradition. Ceramic and stone items survive the passage of time much better than items such as carved wooden objects, baskets, cotton cloth and clothing, and feather cloaks and adornments. Archaeologists find items made of these less durable materials only when they have been preserved under unusual conditions. It can be particularly difficult to determine customary use when we have only a few examples of a particular artifact. For example, excavators found a fortuitously preserved set of elongated, sword-shaped or spatula-like wooden items at a large site with a platform mound. Were they calendar sticks, prayer sticks, scepters, or staffs of authority? Or were they battens, the implements that weavers use to guide

threads on looms? We could better answer these questions if we routinely found such items, say, on top of platform mounds but seldom elsewhere. Then we would guess that the wooden rods served a ritual purpose. If we found them in ordinary people's houses, we might conclude that they had a more mundane use.

Besides trying to understand how the Hohokam used the artifacts they left behind, archaeologists have focused much of their research on understanding how they made them—their technology. They study craft production to investigate questions about economic organization as well as manufacturing processes. Who were these artisans? Were they residents of small settlements, large central villages, or both? Did the same artisans (or groups of artisans in a village) specialize in making marine shell ornaments, pottery, and other crafts? If some Hohokam producers specialized in making certain goods, did they work in small, factorylike workshops, by themselves, or with other members of their households? What social messages did palettes and pottery carry beyond their immediate use? Archaeologists have gained insights into all

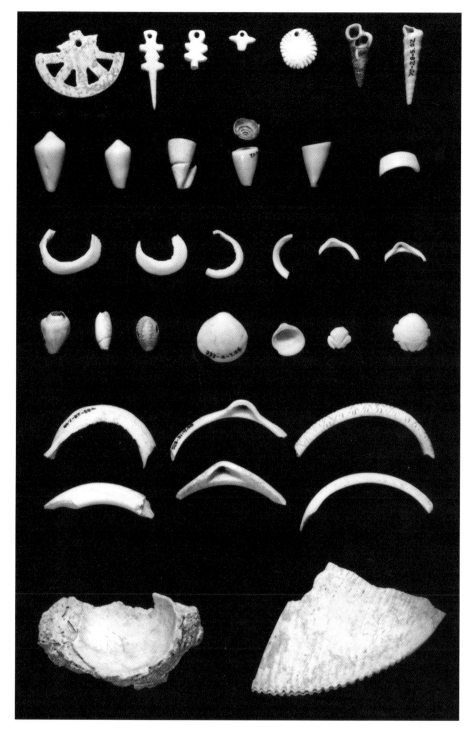

Marine Shell Ornaments

Artisans created a variety of shell ornaments that Hohokam men and women wore in daily life and for ritual gatherings and other special occasions: bracelets, rings, pendants, beads of many sizes and shapes, and small tinkler rattles sewn onto the hems of garments or other flexible materials (fig. 9.4). Archaeologists believe that shellworkers made whole conch shells into trumpets for political and ritual leaders to sound loudly when they summoned their followers or signaled announcements. Such trumpets appear at community center sites with ball courts or platform mounds and in unusually rich burials. Greatly lending credibility to this interpretation, pre-Hispanic Mesoamerican leaders blew shell trumpets, and certain Pueblo priests and village leaders have used them at public events in recent times.

During the Preclassic period (700–1150 CE), many Hohokam people imported a majority of their finished ornaments from shell crafters who lived in the southwesternmost part of Arizona, an area called Papaguería (see map 1), which is relatively near shell

Figure 9.4. Shell items from the Marana Mound site in Tucson include examples in all stages of manufacture.

these questions by examining the objects themselves, carefully noting where they were found, and considering their roles in descendants' cultures. Marine shell ornaments and stone arrow points, artifacts central in my own research, illustrate the study of Hohokam craft traditions.

sources on the Gulf of California in Sonora, Mexico. Some Hohokam settlements in Papaguería are filled with fragments of shell left over from workers' cutting out rough shapes for jewelry and with shell powder from their smoothing and polishing the cut edges. Although artisans in villages of the Phoenix and Tucson Basins also made marine shell ornaments, they imported more finished pieces than they made themselves during these years. In the subsequent Classic period (1150–1450 or 1500), jewelry manufacture in Papaguería declined, and artisans in the Phoenix and Tucson areas, where most of the consumers lived, came to dominate jewelry production.

Archaeologists do not know whether Phoenix and Tucson artisans obtained whole shells by traveling to the Gulf of California or by trading with middlemen in Papaguería who might have journeyed to the coast or, in turn, traded with coastal inhabitants. We think that Hohokam travelers sometimes did journey to distant shell-covered beaches on the gulf, because their nineteenth-century O'odham descendants continued this tradition with coastal expeditions to gather sea salt (see chapter 16). Boulders along foot trails across Papaguería bear petroglyph images of shells, strong clues that Hohokam travelers once followed these paths.

From about 700 CE onward, the Hohokam left plentiful signs of shell crafting, particularly in their houses and their trash dumps. This evidence includes unworked shells, tools for shellworking, partially shaped ornaments, and finished jewelry, which together represent all the stages of manufacture in home villages. To make a large *Glycymeris* shell bracelet, artisans first used a coarse stone abrader to cut around the perimeter of the shell. Then they used granular, cigar-shaped stones to polish the jagged edges of the bracelet (see fig. 7.7). Most bracelets were left unadorned, but makers sometimes incised geometric designs along the margins or carved images of animals such as bighorn sheep and toads on the thickest part of the rim. We find bracelets in many sizes, suggesting that everyone from young children to adults wore them.

Stone Arrow Points

Making arrow points was an important task for hunters who brought down game such as deer with bows and arrows. Some makers of chipped stone tools specialized in arrow points, using high-quality raw materials such as chert and obsidian that allowed them to control the shape and size of the

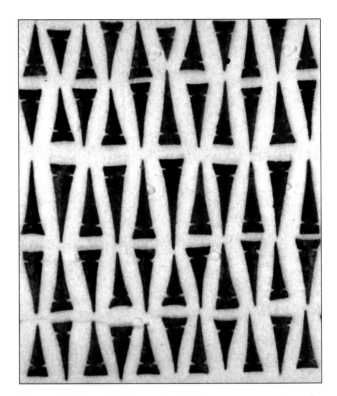

Figure 9.5. Remarkably standardized stone arrow points of the Sedentary period (900–1100 CE) suggest manufacture by highly skilled specialists.

flakes they struck from larger chunks, or "cores." Hohokam artisans especially valued obsidian, a glassy, volcanic stone, because it produced well-shaped arrow points, extremely sharp edges, and superior cutting tools, but the stone was rare in most of the Hohokam homeland. Arrow point makers had to import much of it from distant sources. Steven Shackley, an expert in obsidian sourcing, has perfected methods of chemical analysis that enable him to match pieces from archaeological sites with known natural sources. His studies of chipped stone artifacts reveal that the Hohokam acquired obsidian from more than eight localities across the modern states of Arizona, New Mexico, and Sonora, Mexico.

Hohokam arrow point makers were very skillful, capable of producing intricately chipped points, often in uniform styles (fig. 9.5). They used round stone hammers to strike off smaller pieces of desired sizes and shapes from a larger stone core. They then used wood, bone, or antler tools to remove still smaller flakes, giving the arrow point its final shape. The arrow points recovered at

Snaketown, the large Preclassic site on the Gila River south of Phoenix, show an exceptionally high degree of skill.

Snaketown residents placed several thousand of these stylized points around a few unusual cremation burials. In these cases the points apparently had a ritual function as well as a utilitarian one. The Hohokam also left large numbers of well-made miniature arrow points in and around the platform mounds and walled residential compounds of their Classic period settlements. Why people discarded so many of these unbroken points, even in trash dumps, is a mystery. The Classic period Hohokam likely used whole arrows and arrow points in ritual events, just as Southwestern peoples of more recent times have placed them on altars as offerings and included them as parts of ceremonial attire.

Why Craft Specialization?

Artisans in non-industrial societies may specialize in craft manufacture if they lack adequate farmland on which to live. They can trade the finished goods for basic supplies to support their families. Archaeologists suspect that at least some Hohokam craft specialists turned to craft production to supplement their crops. For example, the Preclassic shell specialists of Papaguería lived in a part of the Sonoran Desert that lacked the year-round rivers and other substantial water sources vital for reliable large-scale farming.

Archaeologists have discovered the largest quantities of valuable craft items, such as obsidian arrow points and shell ornaments, together with evidence for their manufacture, in Hohokam central villages with platform mounds dating to the Classic period. This concentration at community centers suggests that resident leaders might have played influential roles in producing and distributing these valuable goods among widespread consumers. At any rate, when visitors from surrounding settlements attended feasts, religious rituals, or other platform mound events, both craft producers and leaders would have benefited from opportunities for gifting and bartering high-value goods. Worldwide, members of traditional societies prize skilled-craft goods, exotic materials, and items from distant lands. It is probable that aspiring

Hohokam leaders sought to increase their prestige and political power by stockpiling such goods and periodically giving them out to friends and allies.

How Were Craft Goods Circulated?

How exactly did Hohokam artisans benefit economically from their crafts? In one scenario, Hohokam artisans and traders operated within a market system in which supply and demand influenced the relative value of goods. Yet the scarcity of archaeological evidence for market stalls, warehouses, or other tangible remains of markets in Hohokam sites challenges the idea that most goods were exchanged this way (see chapter 10 for an alternative view).

In another scenario, the Hohokam resembled many other non-industrial societies by emphasizing valued crafts in gift giving, paying marriage dowries, gambling, and making ritual offerings. Individuals, families, and villages exchanged gifts to confirm their friendship and loyalty to one another. When a person died, he or she might be buried with high-value goods as a sign of respect or in proportion to his or her social importance and power. Although we cannot document gift giving in the archaeological record, we do have evidence of burial practices. Archaeologists have found differing quantities of high-value offerings in Hohokam burials (see chapter 3). In some traditional societies, a politically powerful person such as a chief or village elder orchestrated the circulation of valuable goods. Archaeologists have as yet found little direct evidence to confirm this kind of craft management among the Hohokam.

Badges of Membership and Symbolic Ornaments

As highly visible and personal objects, ornaments of stone, shell, and bone provide an effective means of communicating social information about people. Particular ornaments could advertise identity and status to close neighbors and people from distant communities alike. Religious and political leaders undoubtedly used objects such as shell trumpets in public rituals to symbolize their power and authority. The ancient Hohokam might also have adorned themselves with recognized kinds of

Figure 9.6. Varied styles of Preclassic period arrow points from Snaketown.

ornaments to signify their economic condition, religious affiliation, or political position.

I believe that Hohokam people, regardless of their age, gender, occupation, and social status, wore marine shell bracelets to advertise their membership in Hohokam culture and society. By doing so, they contrasted themselves with neighboring groups in the southwestern United States, if not with bracelet-wearing peoples to the south in Mexico. Although bracelets also appear among Ancestral Pueblos, the Mogollon, and other peoples of the Southwest, they were scattered and few. Among the Hohokam, they appear regularly in the personal possessions burned during cremations, and they often adorned persons buried in graves. Everywhere we find bracelets made for wearers of all ages. We find higher concentrations of them in centers with platform mounds, lending support to the idea that Hohokam society became more stratified during the Classic period, when mound building flourished. In effect, shell bracelets served as badges of membership, as a tangible and visible way for Hohokam people to assure their contemporaries that they shared values and beliefs.

Shell bracelets were not the only badges of membership in Hohokam society. Hohokam hunters and warriors made distinctive tools and weapons. During the Preclassic period, Hohokam craftsmen shaped arrow points in a variety of distinctive styles (fig. 9.6). Arrow point styles from sites near the city of Gila Bend in west-central Arizona, for example, differ from those at sites in the Phoenix area. The hundreds of arrow points in uniform styles that Snaketown mourners placed beside a few cremated persons must have had widely recognized meanings.

If commonly found craft items can tell us much about Hohokam society, what about rare or special-use forms? Unlike plain shell bracelets, shell pendants carved into stylized toads or frogs, for example, are quite rare. In only a few instances have archaeologists found turquoise mosaic-on-shell pendants (plate 2). During a brief part of the

Preclassic period, Hohokam artisans used an acidic substance made from cactus to etch designs on whole *Glycymeris* shells (plate 1). The highly ornate turquoise and shell pendants and etched objects come only from large villages with ball courts and platform mounds.

Archaeologists can only speculate what shell pendants of frogs or toads, creatures associated with rainy seasons and water, might have symbolized. David Wilcox and Todd Bostwick propose that religious practitioners used frog pendants in agricultural fertility rites designed to bring rain. We can imagine strong incentives for the Hohokam to perform rain-making rites in the desert, where adequate rainfall was a life-and-death matter.

Hohokam artisans also fashioned pointed and polished bone objects, but archaeologists are often uncertain about their function. When we find them placed near the head in a burial, we speculate that they were hairpins (see fig. 3.8) and might have communicated social information about the wearer such as gender, marital status, or membership in a particular organization. Alternatively, the archaeologist Gary Feinman proposes that the Hohokam used these needle-like bone objects in bloodletting rituals, as did the Mayas of southern Mexico.

Crafted goods offer a fascinating portal through which archaeologists can explore many aspects of Hohokam culture and cosmology. We can hope to answer questions about the meaning of Hohokam crafts by carefully testing ideas that begin with archaeological patterns, practices among descendant peoples, or tendencies among producing societies worldwide. After more than a century of research on crafts and craft making, it is truer than ever that much remains to be learned.

James M. Bayman is an associate professor of anthrpology at the University of Hawai`i at Manoa. His archaeological research focuses on the political and economic organization of past societies in the Hawaiian Islands and the southern portion of the US Southwest. He has written extensively on Hohokam craft production.

Figure 10.1. Artist's reconstruction of Pueblo Grande, one of the largest and most complex Hohokam platform mounds, at around 1350.

Irrigation, Production, and Power in Phoenix Basin Hohokam Society

David E. Doyel

In what archaeologists call the Phoenix Basin—the conjoined valleys and confluence areas of the Gila and Salt Rivers and their major tributaries—Hohokam engineers constructed the largest irrigation systems in prehistoric North America. Around these impressive waterworks stretched a heavily populated landscape of villages and monuments. In the lower Salt River valley, for example, where the city of Phoenix now stands, 14 irrigation networks with an estimated aggregate length of 300 miles watered 400 square miles of agricultural land and settlements (fig. 10.2). These engineered landscapes supplied the food that made possible a dense population and a vigorous society. From this core area, significant Hohokam influence reached more than 50,000 square miles across Arizona.

In 1976, when Emil W. (Doc) Haury published his monumental study of Snaketown, *The Hohokam: Desert Farmers and Craftsmen*, archaeologists had studied and reported on only a few of the desert villages. As Haury later noted, new evidence from more sites soon fueled the fire of debate. The thou-

sands of sites documented in the three decades since then reveal a rich regional record that raises questions about some of Haury's basic assumptions regarding the Hohokam and their world—questions about how their society was organized and how it changed over time, about the characteristics of their worldview, and about their economic patterns and expressions of power. As one of Doc's last students, I have observed firsthand the radical changes in archaeologists' thinking about the Hohokam and, indeed, about the nature of Southwestern society.

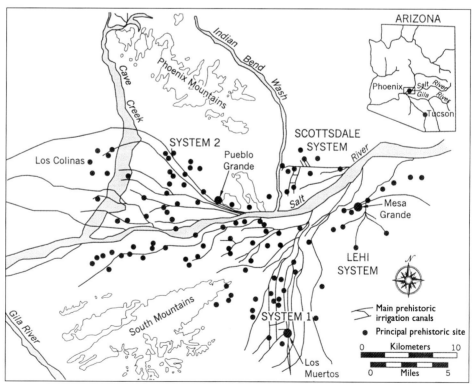

Figure 10.2. Irrigation systems and major settlements along the Salt River in the Phoenix Basin.

When I began working in Arizona, I noticed that Hohokam red-on-buff pottery looked similar wherever I saw it, whether at Gila Bend, Phoenix, Globe, Tucson, or somewhere else. I even saw Hohokam pottery in the juniper- and pine-covered country to the north. The distinctive presence of the sparkly, mica-schist temper specially prepared for making this pottery, along with other production characteristics, suggested a common source or source areas (see chapter 8). The widespread distribution of this pottery puzzled me because it is not durable and breaks easily—which is why we find so much of it on Hohokam sites. It was special nonetheless; many people went to great lengths to obtain some of their own. For centuries this pottery retained strong market value throughout the Hohokam world.

When I published my initial thoughts in the late 1970s, they differed significantly from Haury's. He viewed the Hohokam as a simple, unchanging but talented farming people, with little economic specialization or social stratification. In contrast, I viewed their society as more complex, elaborate, and dynamic. Over time I came to believe that Hohokam Buff Ware was a primary symbol of an expansionist society propelled across the region by a vibrant economic and ideological system. I wondered what type of society could have become so vigorous in a desert environment described by some as "marginal."

That question immediately raises the issue of water management. Because of the Hohokam's long history of irrigation, scholars often cite them in a long-running debate over the relationship between irrigated agriculture and the emergence of complex societies. Some suggest that the engineering, construction, and labor costs of irrigation created a need for centralized management that led to complex bureaucracies and eventually to civilizations. The archaeologist Timothy Earle and I have offered an alternative perspective. It was not the management of irrigation but rather control of agricultural surpluses that provided a foundation that emerging leaders could use to their advantage. But more on this later.

In tandem with their irrigated agriculture, the Hohokam as I imagined them had an organized economy that included merchants, marketplaces, far-reaching trade networks, and entrepreneurs operating within a market-based system, all radical ideas in comparison with Doc's thinking (and see chapter 9 for an alternative view). In time their economy developed into a specialized system of interdependence that enabled Hohokam society to function smoothly despite its complexity. The long-term stability of their economy is a defining characteristic of the Hohokam that sets them apart from their neighbors.

Production and Exchange

Trade, in general, serves many purposes, including circulating resources, people, and ideas and providing social cohesion. The Hohokam traded continuously across the ancient US Southwest and excelled in this arena. How do we know this? Ethnography provides some clues. The historic Akimel O'odham (River People, or Pima), Tohono O'odham (Desert People), and other native peoples commonly distributed food through ceremonies and by trading resources for labor. Writing in the 1930s, the anthropologist Ruth Underhill noted that to acquire corn and wheat from the River People, the Desert People traded goods to them, including cactus seeds, syrup, and fruit; agave hearts, cakes, and fiber; gourds; peppers; acorns; woven sleeping mats and baskets; dried meat from deer and mountain sheep; buckskin; pigments; and salt. They also held ceremonies at which people from better-off villages gave food to residents of villages that had fallen on hard times, creating a tradition of reciprocity. Because the O'odham and Hohokam who preceded them lived in the same environment and shared many traditions (see chapters 14 and 15), we can infer that trade was important to the Hohokam too. The networks of trails across their world, ultimately leading to the northern fringes of Mesoamerica, to California, to the Zuni area of New Mexico, and to the Great Plains, provided many pathways for trade and travel (see fig. 16.2).

Revolutionary advances in analytical techniques for precise chemical and mineralogical sourcing of the raw materials used in Hohokam crafts make it possible to evaluate these ideas closely. We now know that ordinary Hohokam people did not themselves make many of the products they used every day. Consider their pottery. Analysis shows that trade in pottery took place throughout the Hohokam world, and many villages, both within and beyond the core area, produced none of their own red-on-buff pottery or even their own everyday utility wares. Although there were others, the village of Snaketown on the Gila River is probably the best known pottery-making center, located as it is adjacent to one of the largest sources of mica-schist deposits in the region. The occupants of this village were deeply engaged in specialized production and the import-export business (fig. 10.3).

Consider also their grinding tools. The preferred volcanic stone for making thousands of grinding stones, or metates, to process corn comes only from certain mountain formations north of Phoenix and a few other places. Because tooth decay and infection were significant factors in Hohokam mortality, obtaining good-quality stone for metates—stone that left the least possible grit in a family's cornmeal—was important to these farming people. The discovery of manufacturing sites north of Phoenix containing the fragmentary stone residues of metate manufacture, including one site I studied that alone could have produced 4,000 metates, points to a specialized industry and trade. Archaeologists have estimated that 90 percent of the metates at some Phoenix Basin sites came from sources up to 30 miles outside the core area.

In fact, specialists made many of the tools and products used in daily life. Nonperishable goods included tons of marine shells (5,400 shell items came from Haury's second excavation at Snaketown), distinctive arrow points, obsidian (20 source areas have been identified), stone knives and axes, clay figurines, and rare resources such as pigments. Many of the raw materials used were unavailable in the artisans' homeland and had to be acquired by travel, trade, or other means. Many objects for which the Hohokam are best known were produced as personal ornaments. Other items were made for elite persons, to mark their social status. Still others were made especially for rituals and as offerings for the dead, as attested by the hundreds of finely made objects found in burials. The common discovery of exotic items at Hohokam villages shows that

Figure 10.3. Hohokam potters likely transported pottery for trade in much the same way this Tohono O'odham woman carried pots to market in her burden basket in the late 1800s.

imported materials were important to these people and added to their quality of life.

Settlement Patterns, Economy, and Society
We can track the development of Hohokam society by studying its settlement patterns, population growth, architecture, and artifacts. The evidence indicates that over time, Hohokam society became increasingly complex, eventually including chiefdoms, a form of social organization in which power is concentrated in the hands of a single leader. Chiefs conduct ceremonies, settle disputes, and distribute resources; they often live in big houses, wear distinctive clothing, and have greater access to power, wealth, and labor than do ordinary people. They may come from landed families or may lead by charisma, their connection to the gods, or force. Often the position is inherited. Chiefdoms encompass populations in the thousands, complex settlement patterns, and interdependence among villages across the landscape.

Phoenix Basin Hohokam society was organized into simple chiefdoms by 800 or 900 CE. The corresponding settlement pattern consisted of a group of related villages, referred to as a community, that included at least one large, primary settlement featuring one or more ceremonial ball courts. Shared irrigation systems, ceremonies, and marketplaces integrated communities into larger social networks. Large plazas located near the centers of the primary villages served as hubs of public life and sites for the performance of cere-

Figure 10.4. A recurring motif in Hohokam pottery and rock art is a person with a staff carrying a large basket or net bag supported by a tumpline around the forehead. The image shows how market goods might have been transported.

monies and life-cycle rituals. Plazas also served as marketplaces, likely organized according to seasonal and ceremonial schedules. Evidence supporting this idea includes the remains of small structures along the edge of the great plaza at Snaketown that could have served as stalls or stands for itinerant vendors (fig. 10.4).

By 1050 CE the Hohokam had built more than 225 ball courts in villages across southern and central Arizona (map 3). Along the Salt and Gila Rivers, ball court villages were positioned about every three miles, and many lay within a few hours' or a day's round-trip walk from one another. The long, flat valleys of the Hohokam world facilitated travel and trade. To accommodate their growing society, the Hohokam established new villages, some with ball courts, outside the core area. They settled near what is now Prescott, Arizona, in the Verde Valley, farther east along the Mogollon Rim, and in the area that is today the Arizona–New Mexico border. In these places the Hohokam introduced their ball courts, ideology, and artifacts to local people, and from them they traded with the core area.

During the same years, the Chaco culture was expanding to the south out of Chaco Canyon in

northwestern New Mexico, and the two economic powers shared a border along the Little Colorado River valley. The Chaco people traded turquoise and jet to the Hohokam for marine shell and cotton. Hohokam trade networks also extended south into what is now Mexico. Mesoamerican items found in Hohokam sites include approximately 500 copper bells and 100 pyrite-encrusted, sandstone-backed mirrors, likely used by elites to mark their status (see chapter 7). At their peak, Hohokam trade networks extended from the northern outposts of Mesoamerica to Chaco Canyon, with villages strategically located along the trade routes (fig. 10.5).

The chiefs facilitated trade and derived social power from the accomplishments of their followers. Although their ideology seems to have emphasized the preeminence of the community rather than the personal aggrandizement of a leader, we do find evidence of the rising status of leaders in the conspicuous display of prestige objects and the distribution of finely crafted items. For example, most of the elaborate artifacts associated with burials at Snaketown came from only 3 of the 24 cemeteries there. Clearly, some people enjoyed more of these prestigious belongings than others, and their burial

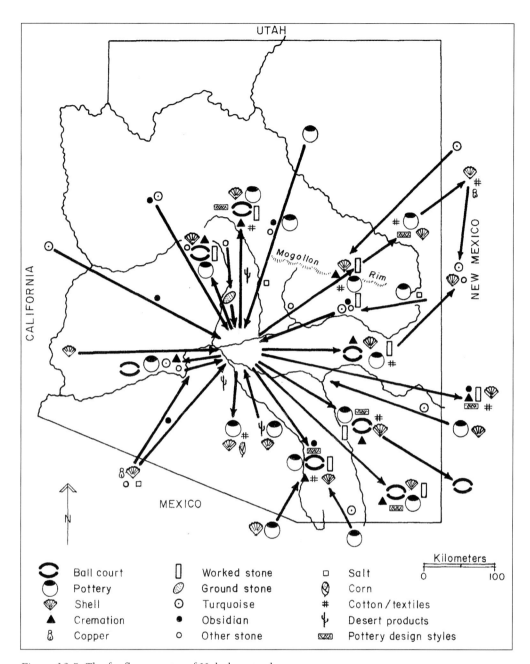

UTAH

CALIFORNIA

Mogollon

Rim

NEW MEXICO

MEXICO

N

Kilometers
0   100

◖◗	Ball court	◖	Worked stone	▫	Salt
◐	Pottery	⬭	Ground stone	⊙	Corn
🐚	Shell	◉	Turquoise	#	Cotton/textiles
▲	Cremation	●	Obsidian	ψ	Desert products
𝟠	Copper	○	Other stone	▨	Pottery design styles

Figure 10.5. The far-flung routes of Hohokam trade.

accompaniments reflected this difference even after death. A cult that I dubbed the "Rainbow Way"—because of its symbolic focus on water, fertility, and life forms and its use of color symbolism and reflective materials—dominated this period.

By 1050 we also find evidence of greater political centralization. A well-known example is Snaketown. Boasting a population of several thousand, with nearly 60 trash mounds, a great plaza, two ball courts, and an early kind of platform mound, this site was a religious, economic, and social center. Surveys beginning in the late 1990s revealed two additional ball court villages along the same irrigation system, one located 3.5 miles to the west and another 5 miles west again. These two villages and their surrounding settlements would have doubled the local population, making the combined Snaketown irrigation community one of the largest polities in North America at that time. Another large irrigation community, known as Grewe, lay across the Gila River and upstream, near Casa Grande.

Why Chiefdoms?

Cross-cultural research shows that the management of even large irrigation systems does not necessarily require the strong central control or bureaucracy typical of state-level governments, contrary to what some scholars had argued. Archaeology is of great value in this debate because it provides opportunities to study individual cultures over long periods of time, and the Hohokam make an excellent case study. We now know that they built large portions of their irrigation systems before the advent of chiefly organization. But with continued growth and expansion, their society became more complex. Tim Earle and I believe that it was the chiefs' control over agricultural surpluses, beyond what a community needed to feed itself, and their ability to direct the subsequent use of these products that financed the emerging chiefdoms—not management of the irrigation systems. The chiefly families might have accumulated large stores by controlling the best land and laying claim to canal lines and other agricultural infrastructure in the landscape to justify their demands for "rent" or tribute. Chiefs in larger communities with the potential to produce surpluses could mobilize wealth to finance their power and ambitions. Eventually, buildings and monuments materially marked their claims to ownership.

But why would farmers who invested hard labor in their irrigation systems decide to pay rent or tribute to support emerging leaders? It seems that they had little choice. To leave, or "vote with their feet," would have meant losing rights to their holdings. Irrigation farmers were essentially tied to their assets, which made them easy targets for emerging elites. In some chiefdoms, warriors in the service of a chief have controlled the most productive land, but we need more research to assess whether this might have been the case among the Hohokam.

A Time of Change

The Classic period (1150–1540 or 1500) was a time of change across the Southwest. Among the Hohokam, some ancestral marketplaces and produc-

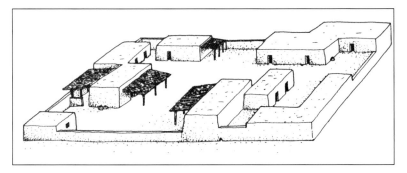

Figure 10.6. During the Classic period, the adobe room clusters of one to several households were enclosed in a walled residential compound.

tion centers, such as Snaketown, lost population while other communities grew larger. For example, by 1300 the Casa Grande (Grewe) irrigation community had consolidated formerly separate canal lines into a single irrigation system encompassing five platform mound villages along a canal 21 miles long that watered 15,000 acres. The Lehi irrigation community in present-day Mesa, Arizona, had 21 miles of trunk-line canals and 14,000 acres of fields (see fig. 10.2). A pattern in which smaller sets of communities consolidated into larger, combined ones dominated this period. Ultimately, each of the largest Phoenix Basin irrigation communities supported 6,000 to 10,000 people.

Classic Hohokam society developed during a time of unstable environmental conditions and scarce resources. One theory is that floods altered the river channels and undermined the canal networks, and indeed, the reconfiguration of the irrigation systems at this time may have been partly in response to such changes (see chapter 11). For example, before the Classic period, seven ball court communities averaged 2,700 acres of irrigated land along the middle Gila River near Snaketown. In the Classic period, these communities consolidated into three larger irrigation communities with more than 5,000 acres of irrigated land each.

As part of this reorganization, the Hohokam altered their built environment to signal fundamental changes in their society. The open village plans of earlier times—the ball courts and large plazas—gave way to walled compounds and elevated platform mounds (figs. 10.6, 10.7). More than 100 platform mounds, towers, and great houses, probably brightly decorated, served as temples, observa-

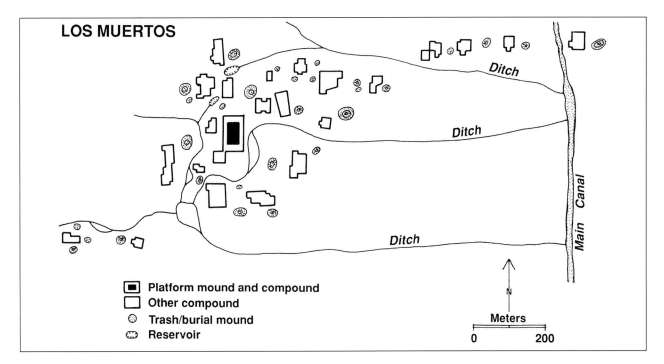

tories, elite residences, and symbols of power. The compounds and high walls suggest an exclusionary social order and hint at intimidation and control. These changes likely brought a new system of property rights, a primary objective of which was to extract surpluses from farmers' harvests through control over irrigation. The buildings and monuments and their spatial relationships encoded this new social order onto the landscape through an ideology I call the "Power Way" because of the consolidation of power by the leadership.

Another sign of the transformation taking place in Hohokam society is the disappearance of much of the familiar Hohokam ritual paraphernalia before the early Classic period. Gone were the palette-and-censer ceremonial complex and related kinds of finely crafted items. Some specialized craft production did continue into this period. For example, David Abbott estimates that residents of Pueblo Grande imported 70 percent of the slipped red pottery archaeologists have found there. This polished red pottery and later polychrome wares replaced the once prized buff ware. Some craft arts, including the marine shell industry, remained of

high quality, probably representing symbols associated with status, rank, and ritual. Even mortuary patterns changed significantly as the old Rainbow Way yielded to new symbols.

We are uncertain why Classic period culture disappeared, but environmental disturbances likely played a key role. Whatever the case, without surplus crops from their irrigated fields, the Hohokam of the Phoenix Basin could not sustain their elaborate society. When Spaniards entered the area in the late 1600s, the massive irrigation systems lay abandoned. Several centuries later, the canals the Hohokam built would serve as a foundation for the people who inhabit the region today, as a new Phoenix rose from the ashes of Hohokam civilization. If modern Phoenix and Tucson survive to the year 3000, they will have matched the Hohokam's tenure in the Arizona desert.

David E. Doyel earned his PhD in anthropology at the University of Arizona, where Emil Haury chaired his doctoral committee. He has devoted his professional career to the study of Southwestern archaeology and to museum development and administration.

Figure 11.1. Aerial view of Snaketown and today's desert landscape along the dammed and dry Gila River.

Changing Views of Snaketown in a Larger Landscape

John C. Ravesloot

The collapsed walls of test trenches in several of Snaketown's 60 trash mounds were all that remained of Emil Haury's excavations when I first visited the site in 1975 with fellow archaeologists. We had been investigating sites in New River, Arizona, on the northern periphery of the Hohokam culture area, and had made the trip south to see this famous National Historic Landmark Site and Casa Grande Ruins National Monument on our day off. Standing on the edge of the large ball court of this ancient village, we found it difficult to visualize how Snaketown might have looked during its heyday, when generations of people, a thousand or more at a time, lived on this terrace above the Gila River. Snaketown's name originated not with these former inhabitants, however, but with the Akimel O'odham (River People), commonly known as the Pima, who established a modern village on the site in the 1870s and called their home "Skoaquick," Place of the Snakes.

Emil Haury and Harold Gladwin's excavations at Snaketown in 1934–35 provided the data that allowed archaeologists to establish the first chronology of Hohokam culture and demonstrated that the Hohokam lived in permanent villages, had regular contact with Mesoamerican societies, and maintained far-reaching trade networks to acquire shell from the Pacific and Gulf of California coasts. The decorated red-on-buff pottery, elaborate shell and stone carvings, and turquoise mosaics that archaeologists uncovered as they excavated Hohokam settlements testified to the well-developed artistic abilities of these farming people. They were also capable engineers who constructed ball courts, plat-form mounds, and remarkable canal systems to water their fields.

Gladwin and Haury's early work launched archaeologists' efforts to understand the Hohokam cultural tradition, but many questions remained unanswered. Where had these people come from? How long had they been sedentary farmers along the Gila River? How socially and politically complex was their society? Why was Snaketown abandoned around 1100 CE, after a thousand years of village life? Seeking answers to these questions, Emil Haury revisited Snaketown in 1964–65 to begin a new program of excavations 30 years after his initial work there.

Our visit to Casa Grande, with its visible buildings and interpretive trails, contrasted sharply with the visit to Snaketown, which sits devoid of standing walls, isolated on the Gila River Indian Reservation. The great house for which Casa Grande ("big house" in Spanish) is named served populations and settlements along the middle Gila River during the Classic period, after Snaketown had been abandoned, at least in Haury's view. Casa Grande residents built their multistoried great house around 1350 but ultimately abandoned it by the late 1400s.

As a newcomer to Hohokam archaeology, I remember wondering what events or processes had triggered the abandonment of ancestral villages such as Snaketown and the eventual collapse of Hohokam society. Were environmental factors such as drought, alkali buildup in the fields caused by centuries of irrigation, and destruction of the mesquite groves along the river to blame? Did a hundred-year flood of the Gila River touch off a

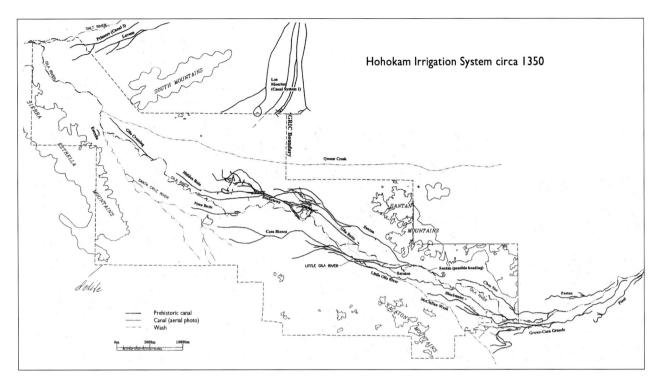

Figure 11.2. Hohokam canal lines in the vicinity of the present-day Gila River Indian Community.

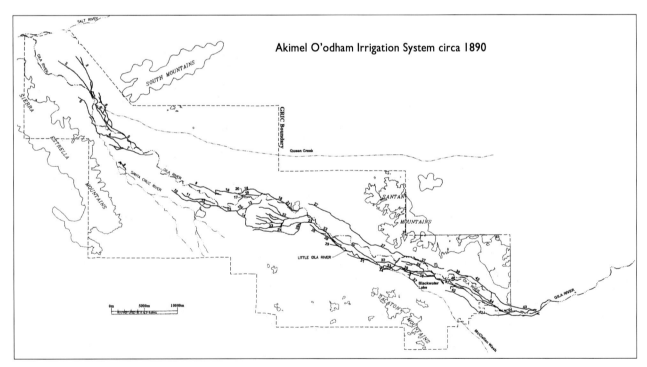

Figure 11.3. Historic Akimel O'odham canal lines in the vicinity of the Gila River Indian Community.

downward spiral? I pondered what other factors might have been to blame, such as warfare and disease. Did the abandonment of villages take place slowly over several generations or rapidly because the Hohokam people had too little time to react and adapt to changing environmental and social conditions? Questions such as these have intrigued researchers for more than a century, and after my

Figure 11.4. The construction of Coolidge Dam in 1924 put an end to the natural flow of the Gila River.

of the river. The contemporary desert conditions result from the upstream diversion of water on the Gila River by non-Indian farmers in the 1880s, together with drought. Both crippled Pima farming. Then, in 1924, the construction of Coolidge Dam near San Carlos, Arizona, ended irrigation agriculture as it had been practiced on the Gila River for nearly 2,000 years (fig. 11.4).

The intent of the Pima-Maricopa Irrigation Project, funded by the United States Bureau of Reclamation, Department of the Interior, was to provide the Gila River Indian Community with the dependable supply of water it had lost to upstream diversion and Coolidge Dam. The environmental studies required by federal law enabled the Community's cultural resources program to document and study Hohokam and historic Pima sites that would be affected by the construction of new concrete-lined canals, protective channels, dikes, and reservoirs.

In 10 years of archaeological surveying, we covered more than 150,000 acres of the reservation and recorded 1,000 sites representing nearly 5,000 years of occupation, from the Middle Archaic period (beginning about 3000 BCE) through the historic period (roughly 1700–1950). This survey of the middle Gila River valley supplied important details about Hohokam land-use strategies—details otherwise unavailable in central Arizona, where modern urban development makes it impossible to conduct a systematic study of surface remains. Our goal was to reconstruct the landscape in which the Hohokam had lived. That landscape possessed not only physical characteristics such as topography and natural resources but also cultural properties—the ways people used it for subsistence, social interaction, and ideological or ceremonial purposes. The information we gathered enabled us to place Snaketown within its broader context of Hohokam society and to see it once again as the center of a living community.

Before the Gila River survey, we knew little about the history of land use outside the archaeologically defined boundaries of Snaketown. Emil Haury had conducted excavations at several Classic period compounds to the west, but his studies were

visits to Snaketown and Casa Grande in 1975, they fascinated me as well.

My next opportunity to visit Snaketown came in 1993, when I accepted the position of founding director of the Gila River Indian Community's Cultural Resource Management Program, which I held until 2005. The Community established a cultural resources program as part of its planning to construct a modern system to deliver water to 146,000 acres of land for agricultural, recreational, and commercial purposes. The Pima-Maricopa Irrigation Project was planned to consist of 82 miles of main-stem canals and 2,400 miles of secondary canals. Its designers laid out the canals to follow the alignment and slope of the ancient Hohokam canals and to use gravity in the same way.

Like the Hohokam, their Akimel O'odham, or Pima, descendants built and maintained large canal irrigation systems along the Gila and Salt Rivers to water their crops of corn, beans, squash, and cotton (figs. 11.2, 11.3). In the 1850s, Pima farmers using canals they had built atop the prehistoric ones produced huge surpluses of corn and wheat that they sold to the US military and to immigrants heading for California. Today the mighty Gila River is dry except after winter storms and summer rains. Gone is the lush habitat with its cottonwoods, cattails, arrow weed, and mesquite groves lining the banks

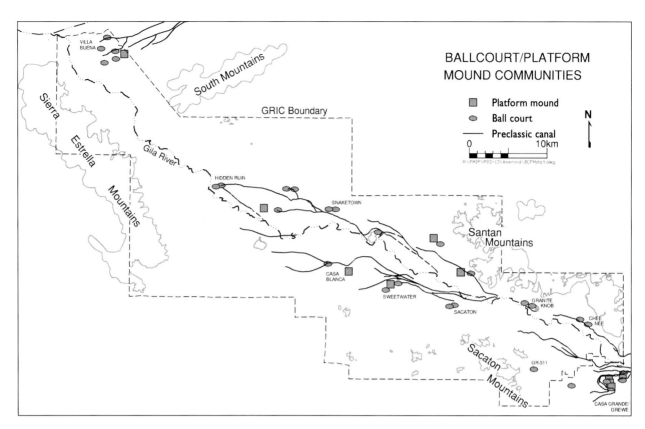

Figure 11.5. Sites with ball courts and platform mounds in the Gila River Indian Community.

limited and did not include recording sites in the vicinity of Snaketown. It is unsurprising, then, that Haury's understanding of Snaketown's abandonment at 1100 was inadequate, for he viewed the village in isolation from the larger middle Gila River landscape. Thanks to our survey and other work at Hohokam sites, we now know that Haury's ideas about the transition from the Preclassic to the Classic period were inaccurate, and we are rethinking the trajectory of Hohokam cultural development.

The survey told us that many Hohokam villages stood on either side of the 250-acre Snaketown site, along the second terrace of the Gila River in a surrounding area stretching six miles upriver and downriver and as much as two miles inland. Within this landscape we found main, distribution, and lateral canals, hundreds of mounded trash and architectural deposits, compounds, rock piles, roasting pits, and two new ball courts (plate 18). People lived in the area from the late Archaic period through the Hohokam Preclassic and Classic periods and up to today. None of the settlements we found was as large or impressive as Snaketown,

which was undoubtedly the focal point of this irrigation community during Preclassic times. But we now know that Snaketown was also the focal point of an even larger entity—a regional ball court system.

Boasting two ball courts, Snaketown was one of the largest and most important community centers on the middle Gila River, but it was far from the only one. During our survey we documented 28 ball courts at 15 settlements (fig. 11.5). They stood along four canal systems, known as Canal System 3, Santan-Snaketown, Chee Nee–Granite Knob, and Casa Blanca. We even found a ball court village away from the Gila on the eastern slope of the Sacaton Mountains.

Our survey also changed the way we understood the abandonment of Snaketown. It seems that after 1100, the people who lived there and in neighboring villages did not leave the area but reorganized themselves into fewer but larger platform mound communities. By 1150, the beginning of the Classic period, the number of centers with public buildings along the middle Gila had fallen to six, on three different canal systems, down from the previous 15 ball court sites. People were similarly aggregating in larger villages all across the Southwest at this time. In the Hohokam area, the consolidation of shorter canal systems into fewer but longer lines also contributed to the restructuring of many Pre-classic villages into a few larger complexes. The growth and consolidation of irrigation communities in the Classic period on the middle Gila are best illustrated by the history of the Santan-Snaketown canal system.

During the Pioneer period—the beginning of the Hohokam sequence—people in the area surrounding Snaketown began building four short canals controlled from separate headgates at Pima Butte, Gila Butte, Diversion Point Two, and Olberg Butte. We now know that they abandoned the canal heading at Pima Butte by the end of the Colonial period and extended the Snaketown canal westward to bring water to another large Preclassic village, Hidden Ruin. It is also likely that sometime during the Sedentary period they extended one or more of the Santan canal alignments to provide water to a cluster of settlements around Gila Butte. The canal line heading from Diversion Point Two seems to have continued in use, but it probably saw no flow during dry years.

By roughly 1000 CE, middle Gila residents near Snaketown had consolidated the original four canal lines into two systems. Later, during the Classic period, they lengthened several branches of the Santan canal westward and linked them to the Snaketown canal. It seems that the integration of the four short canal systems into a single Santan-Snaketown irrigation system over time increased the reliability of water for farmers, opened up new fields, and led to the relocation of some settlements.

The fields associated with the four initial, separate canal systems ranged in size from 1,165 acres watered from the Pima Butte headgate to 2,400 acres for the Diversion Point Two headgate. On average these canals each watered 1,750 acres. By the late Sedentary period, around 1050 CE, 18,900 acres of land lay in the irrigated zones. The total area under irrigation declined by 2,400 acres in the Classic period, about 1300 CE, to 16,500 acres, but the average irrigated acreage per settlement with platform mounds more than doubled, to 5,500

acres. The consolidation of the four small canal lines into the final Santan-Snaketown system accompanied a decrease in the number of settlements possessing public architecture, from seven settlements with 10 ball courts in Preclassic times to just three settlements with platform mounds in the Classic period.

Why did the people living along the final, Classic period Santan-Snaketown irrigation system consolidate their canals and reorganize themselves on the landscape? I believe that recent geomorphic studies of the Gila River by Michael Waters and me offer at least a partial explanation.

During much of the Hohokam occupation of the middle Gila River valley, the river was aggrading—that is, soil deposits were accumulating on the riverbed rather than eroding away. The river occasionally overflowed its banks, which added to the buildup of the river terraces. Water flowed year-round and was confined to the narrow river channel except during floods. The predictable stream flow provided excellent conditions for the establishment of canal systems. But toward the end of the Preclassic period, after many years of floodplain stability and predictable stream flow, Hohokam farmers faced an environmental catastrophe. Sometime between 1020 and 1160, the Gila River underwent a dramatic change as it cut down into the floodplain and became much wider, more like the river channel we see today (fig. 11.6). This downcutting would have made many Hohokam canal headgates unusable and forced irrigators to rely on fewer locations for water intake, triggering the rebuilding of canals and the loss of cultivated land.

The disastrous events along the Gila coincided with the organizational changes we see in the Hohokam archaeological record between the Preclassic and Classic periods. Between 1050 and 1150, people moved from long-occupied villages such as Snaketown and resettled in growing communities nearby. By 1250 a new organizational structure had emerged, consisting of fewer but larger settlements along consolidated canal systems. Platform mounds replaced ball courts, and material and ritual aspects of culture also changed (see chapters 6 and 10). Increased demands for labor to realign and operate irrigation systems

Figure 11.6. The mighty Gila River in 1915.

might have led to this consolidation, along with new ways of interacting for maintenance and water allocation.

The new Classic period organization sustained itself until around 1400 or 1450, when Hohokam culture as defined by archaeologists collapsed, and inhabitants left the remaining villages and canal systems. Again, environmental changes may have played a central role. Fred Nials and his colleagues propose that a period of droughts and heavy floods in the mid-1300s seriously affected the canals. Charles Redman and his associates conclude that Hohokam society was insufficiently resilient to cope with both serious floods and droughts. To the contrary, Michael Waters and I suggest that Hohokam farmers capably responded to floods and droughts of all magnitudes for more than a millennium. We believe instead of finally succumbing to floods, the Hohokam of the late Classic period could not withstand the unusually prolonged period of low river flow from 1450 to 1870, when consistently less water was available than at any time in the previous thousand years.

We do not know how the people who continued to live along the Gila River and elsewhere in the Hohokam homeland after the collapse organized themselves, although the historic Pima Indians show many continuities with the Hohokam. I believe that the Hohokam entered a new developmental period as a result of the declining availability of water starting about 1450, when large populations could no longer support themselves. Rather than a record of environmental disaster and demise, the history of farming in the middle Gila River valley from Hohokam through Pima times (fig. 11.7)—farming that continues today with the Pima-Maricopa Irrigation Project—demonstrates the long-term resilience of these people and the sustainability of their irrigation systems.

Figure 11.7. With the cessation of river flow, mechanized irrigation at a reduced scale replaced riverine canals in the middle Gila Valley.

John Ravesloot was director of the Gila River Indian Community's Cultural Resource Management Program for 12 years. There he oversaw a large regional survey and related excavations and coordinated the construction of the Huhugam Cultural Center. He is now a principal at William Self Associates in Tucson, with research interests including settlement patterns, landscape archaeology, geoarchaeology, and mortuary analysis.

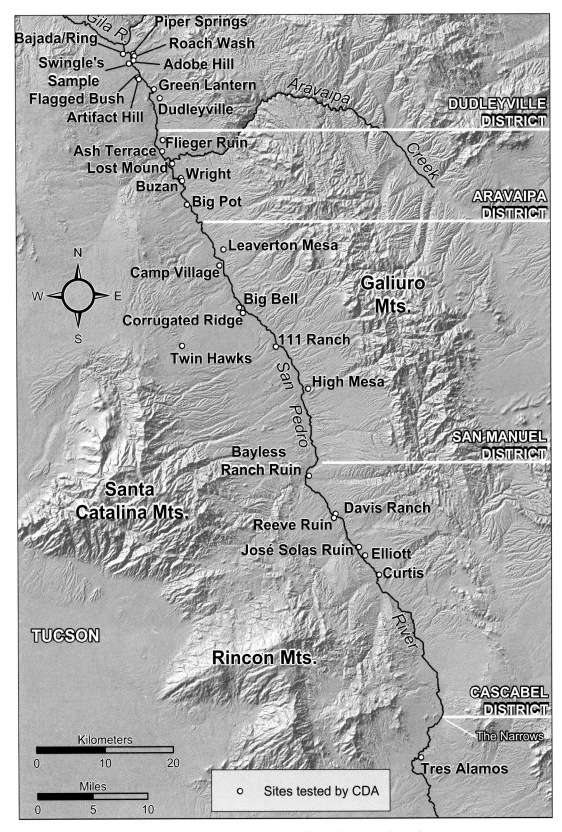

Figure 12.1. Excavated sites in the northern San Pedro Valley, with district boundaries.

A San Pedro Valley Perspective on Ancestral Pueblo Migration in the Hohokam World

Jeffery J. Clark

Cool water on parched lips. Green fields blanketing the valley floor. Some had argued that the treacherous descent into this sun-seared land was a fool's quest. But the scouts had been right. Nestled between the mountains were rivers that raced through canyons only to be tamed by the people who lived in the valleys. We could begin a new life in this land, but what about these strange people? We have traded with them in the past. Will they accept us as neighbors in our time of need?

These might have been some of the thoughts and sensations experienced by Ancestral Pueblo migrants to Hohokam lands in the late thirteenth century. The Colorado Plateau had been stricken by a drought that had devastated their rain-fed crops. The social unrest that followed led many families and even entire villages to migrate toward rivers and springs that offered permanent water. The migrations left the Kayenta region in northeastern Arizona almost completely depopulated and played an important role in reshaping the fourteenth-century Southwest. Some migrants reached the river valleys of central and southeastern Arizona, where they settled among people archaeologists call the Hohokam (fig. 12.3). The effects of this diaspora reverberated across the Hohokam world for a century, leaving behind a confusing pattern of artifacts and architecture that has vexed Southwest archaeologists for nearly as long.

Although the Hohokam world was large and diverse, its inhabitants shared many values, engaged

in similar economic and ritual activities, and probably spoke mutually intelligible languages. They practiced intensive irrigation agriculture that tethered them to their land and fostered a strong sense of community and territory. Ancestral Pueblo migrants had very different life-styles and spoke different languages. These foreigners must have been a source of both fascination and alarm as they arrived in increasing numbers, bringing with them highly developed traditions of pottery and textile manufacture. The archaeology of every river valley in southern

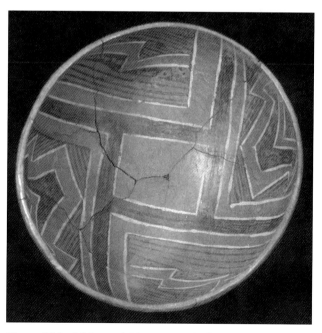

Figure 12.2. A Maverick Mountain Polychrome bowl made by an immigrant Kayenta potter living in southern Arizona.

Arizona tells a different tale of how immigrants and locals struggled to get along—or simply struggled. These stories form one of the most intriguing passages in the history of the prehistoric Southwest.

The Northern San Pedro Valley

The northern San Pedro Valley, roughly 300 miles south of the Kayenta region, was one of the more remote areas to which Ancestral Pueblos relocated. Although today a journey between the two places takes five hours by car, it would have been a daunting undertaking for pre-Hispanic migrants, who traveled on foot without pack animals or wheeled conveyances. They probably made the journey in stages, moving from valley to valley, building temporary shelters, trading with local people, and "testing the waters" for opportunities to stay. In many regards, the San Pedro Valley was the end of the line. Although it was less fertile than closer destinations such as the Safford Basin and the Tonto Basin, it was also less populated. In addition, its inhabitants had a reputation for accepting new people and new ideas.

Today the San Pedro is the last undeveloped river valley in the Sonoran Desert (see plate 15). The Santa Catalina and Rincon Mountains have been effective barriers to urban sprawl from the adjacent Tucson Basin. The absence of modern settlements has allowed archaeologists to reconstruct the history of indigenous settlement and culture development there at a scale impossible for other valleys in the region.

The Center for Desert Archaeology has con-

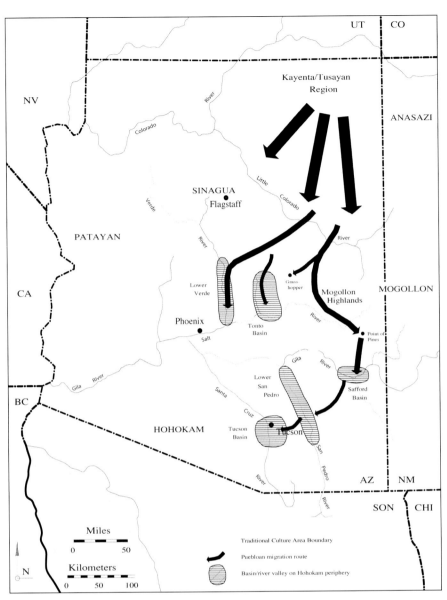

Figure 12.3. Ancestral Pueblo migration routes into central and southern Arizona in the late 1200s and 1300s.

ducted research in the northern San Pedro Valley since 1990, focusing on the cobble and adobe ruins of Classic period settlements. Archaeologists tested trash mounds at 29 sites to obtain artifacts and environmental samples. Such information can tell us who lived in these settlements and how they made their living. Using information gained from these test excavations and earlier large-scale efforts by the Amerind Foundation, we can divide the northern San Pedro Valley into districts based primarily on who lived there—local populations or in-migrating Ancestral Pueblos (fig. 12.1).

Ball Courts, Buff Wares, and Beyond

To understand the repercussions the Ancestral Pueblo migrants created in their new home, we must first reconstruct the lifeways and cultural history of the local inhabitants. Who were the indigenous groups living in the San Pedro Valley before and during the Classic period? Like groups elsewhere in southern Arizona, the Preclassic (700–1150 CE) inhabitants of the northern San Pedro were influenced by people in the Phoenix Basin, the so-called Hohokam heartland.

The northern San Pedro Valley lies near the eastern margin of what archaeologists have called the Hohokam culture area, the region in which we find remnants of the architecture, pottery, and other artifacts that are distinctively Hohokam. The people living on the margins of this area display some but not all of the features of Hohokam culture.

For example, the people of the northern San Pedro Valley constructed many Hohokam-style ball courts (plate 13). Yet we find Middle Gila Buff Ware, a typical Hohokam type of pottery, and Hohokam-style elaborate cremation burials only in what we call the Aravaipa and Dudleyville districts, areas nearest the Gila River. Groups in these districts imported Middle Gila Buff Ware from the Phoenix Basin and also made a sophisticated imitation tempered with a distinctive mineral from an outcropping in the Aravaipa district. This area exhibited the strongest Phoenix Basin influence during the Preclassic and Classic periods.

Moving south along the river, both imported and local imitations of Middle Gila Buff Ware give way to red-on-brown pottery painted in a variety of styles that reflect local decorative traditions and Mogollon traditions borrowed from groups to the east. In the San Manuel district, we find ceramics showing Hohokam and local influences in roughly equal proportions. In the Cascabel district, local design styles dominate alongside large ball courts that show a Hohokam influence. It appears that centuries before the arrival of Ancestral Pueblo migrants during the thirteenth century, the inhabitants of the northern San Pedro Valley were not a homogeneous cultural group. They included both Phoenix Basin migrants and local people who accepted Hohokam ideology in varying degrees.

The houses people live in and the tools and ornaments they use every day tend to be more reliable indicators of cultural background than are patterns associated with rituals and public events. As a result, we can identify the probable origins of the people living in the San Pedro Valley by peeking into their pantries and sifting through their trash as we excavate. We learn much about the private lives of ancient people this way, including how they built their houses, organized their domestic space, and prepared their food. These are behaviors that often differ among cultures.

During the Preclassic period, many of the inhabitants of southern Arizona made distinctive pithouses. The locations of wall posts on the pithouse floor and a shallow groove running around the perimeter, where smaller branches were placed, show us that these structures were literally "houses in pits." In this Hohokam construction style, house walls were built inside the pit, rising upward from its bottom. Many other groups in the Southwest, including early Ancestral Pueblos, built "true" pithouses that instead used the edge of the pit as the lower portion of the wall. Other distinctive features of Hohokam houses in pits were wide-ramped entries and circular hearths that the builders deliberately hardened by exposing them to intense heat in a process similar to ceramic firing.

Hohokam settlements were arranged in courtyard groups, usually with two or three structures facing onto a common area. Courtyard groups were the architectural building blocks of large villages and were inhabited by some fundamental social unit such as an extended family. Carefully studied Preclassic settlements throughout the northern San Pedro Valley suggest that pithouse villages there followed this Hohokam template.

We do not see quite the same arrangements in all parts of the San Pedro Valley, however. Excavated pithouses in the Aravaipa district, where Hohokam ceramic decoration and burial practices prevail, are almost exclusively houses in pits, just as in the Phoenix Basin. Settlements in the San Manuel and Cascabel districts contain both houses in pits and true pithouses of local style. Sometimes we find both types of structures in the same courtyard group. This mixture of styles supports the view that

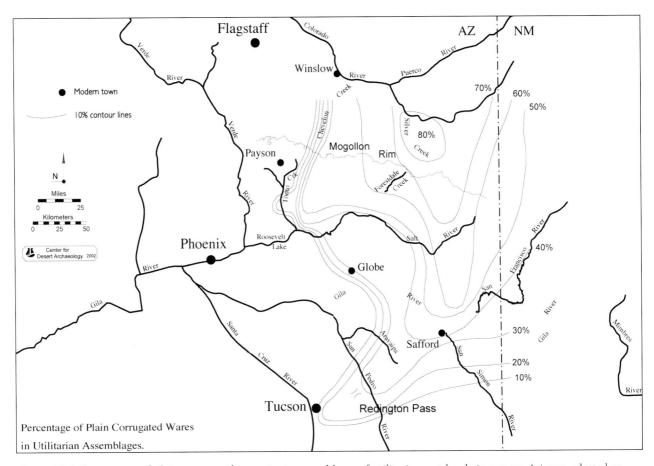

Modern town

10% contour lines

N

Miles
0   25
Kilometers
0   25   50

Center for
Desert Archaeology 2002

Percentage of Plain Corrugated Wares
in Utilitarian Assemblages.

Figure 12.4. Percentages of plain corrugated ceramics in assemblages of utilitarian potsherds in eastern Arizona, plotted as isobars.

Hohokam influence gradually gave way to local traditions farther south along the San Pedro River.

During the late eleventh century, people in the Phoenix Basin abruptly stopped building and using ball courts, indicating that this important institution and the ideology and practices associated with it fell out of favor in the heartland. Reasons for this sudden demise have yet to be ascertained (see chapters 6 and 10). At roughly the same time, the export of Middle Gila Buff Ware from the Phoenix Basin to other valleys fell sharply. Cremation burial continued, but with fewer, less elaborate grave offerings. Several of the most important villages lost population, suggesting serious disruption in Preclassic Hohokam society in the Phoenix Basin (see chapter 11).

These dramatic changes rippled through other river valleys in southern Arizona, including the San Pedro, where local imitations of Middle Gila Buff

Ware also ceased to be made. In its place, people began to rely almost exclusively on locally made plain ware pottery. Many of the villages in the northern San Pedro Valley declined in population, and groups spread out through the valley, establishing many small farmsteads. Because these people made or imported so little decorated pottery that can be dated to this era, we have a hard time identifying such sites. Many residents continued to live in courtyard groups, cremate their dead, and build houses in pits within these smaller settlements. In other words, domestic life remained unchanged despite the collapse of larger social institutions. Many San Pedro groups, particularly those in the Dudleyville and Aravaipa districts, continued to have strong ties to the Phoenix Basin. Yet the entire region was probably socially and economically independent, a pattern that continued into the thirteenth century.

Migrants, Mounds, and More

We can trace at least two distinct migrations from the Ancestral Pueblo region into the San Pedro Valley during the Hohokam Classic period. The first took place during the late twelfth and early thirteenth centuries, and the second during the late thirteenth and early fourteenth centuries.

How can we see these migrations in the archaeological record? A sharp increase in "corrugated" pottery at many sites in southeastern Arizona announces the arrival of Puebloan newcomers toward the end of the 1100s. In this kind of pottery, the maker leaves the clay coils incompletely smoothed on the vessel's exterior, giving it a bumpy, or corrugated, look. People used corrugated ware for storage and cooking throughout the Ancestral Pueblo world. As a result, it is ubiquitous in sites on the Colorado Plateau and immediately below the Mogollon Rim. During the early 1200s, the distribution of corrugated pottery reached southward, poking a finger into the northeastern flank of the Hohokam world. This finger extends through the Safford Basin and the San Pedro Valley and ends abruptly in the northeastern Tucson Basin (fig. 12.4). In the northern San Pedro Valley, nearly all the corrugated pottery appears in the San Manuel district, where it amounts to nearly 50 percent of the pottery at some sites. Sites in the Aravaipa district, by contrast, contain less than 5 percent corrugated ware. We know that people in this region were not importing this Puebloan-style pottery from the north, because it was made using sand from local washes as temper.

Thus, Ancestral Pueblo potters and probably their families were moving into settlements in the San Manuel district in the early 1200s. The most likely origin of these people was the Mogollon highlands in east-central Arizona, which were experiencing scant rainfall during this period. In addition to corrugated pottery, we begin to see the use of stone as a construction material at this time, but few other changes appear. The inhabitants of the valley remained dispersed in farmsteads, and local San Manuel settlements rapidly assimilated the immigrants. This district had experienced a great deal of interaction between local and Phoenix Basin groups during the Preclassic period, suggesting that the residents had a tradition of tolerance for new people.

These first relatively small movements heralded a social and economic maelstrom soon to follow. By the late thirteenth century, people from the drought-stricken Kayenta region were undertaking long-distance migrations into the San Pedro Valley. Unlike previous immigrants from the Hohokam heartland and the Mogollon highlands, many Kayenta families either refused or were not allowed to assimilate into local communities. Instead, they formed enclaves in the Cascabel district, where they continued to practice many of the domestic and ritual activities of their homeland. Their attempt to replicate life back home in a new land, and their separation from the local population, makes them relatively easy to find in the archaeological record, once the archaeologist recognizes the telltale markers.

The Amerind Foundation excavated the most conspicuous enclaves, Reeve Ruin and Davis Ranch Ruin, in the 1950s. Both sites displayed domestic architecture and artifacts similar to those of the Kayenta region. Two of the most compelling markers were perforated plates and distinctive hearths built in conjunction with slab-lined entry boxes at the doorways of rooms (fig. 12.5). The entry box, consisting of two low slabs of stone on either side of the entrance and a taller slab in the middle, might have served to trap the sand that frequently blew into houses from dunes in the Kayenta region. They were of little use in the San Pedro Valley, and indeed, a generation after their arrival the immigrants stopped building these. We think that Kayenta potters used the perforated plates (fig. 12.6) as slow wheels to make their exquisitely decorated pottery. In the San Pedro Valley, such plates are common in the Cascabel district but are seldom found outside it. Kayenta migrants also attempted to re-create their ceremonial life, building the kivas, or ceremonial chambers, of their homeland (fig. 12.8). The highly defensible location of Reeve Ruin, situated on a steep ridge and fortified by walls, indicates that relations with local groups were not always cordial.

Shortly after the arrival of the first Kayenta groups, the locals radically altered their lifeways.

Families that had been scattered across the landscape for 200 years came together to build cobble and adobe villages enclosed by walls, perhaps in part because they were suspicious of the newcomers who refused to conform to local traditions. In the San Manuel and Aravaipa districts, people built platform mounds in many villages. These probably served a ceremonial function at some point during their use. Every local village of any significance in the northern San Pedro Valley built a platform mound during the Classic period. Unsurprisingly, we find no mounds in the migrant-dominated Cascabel district. In addition to providing a setting for village rituals, platform mounds might have served as important territorial markers for local groups, symbolizing their seniority in the region and their rights to the best farmland.

Kayenta immigrants were also responsible for notable changes in the kinds of artifacts archaeologists find in both migrant and local settlements. After a hiatus of 200 years, people of the San Pedro Valley once again began to produce decorated ceramics. The Kayenta newcomers produced what archaeologists call Maverick Mountain–style pottery, which closely followed the stylistic traditions of their homeland (see fig. 12.2). Perhaps in reaction, local groups in the Aravaipa district began producing San Carlos Red-on-brown, pottery painted in a local style and tempered with the same mineral formerly used in the red paint of local imitations of Middle Gila Buff Ware during the Preclassic period (fig. 12.7).

During the early 1300s, a new ceramic tradition called Salado Polychrome (plate 6) nearly replaced both Maverick Mountain pottery and San Carlos Red-on-brown. Technologically and stylistically, this tradition closely resembles Ancestral Pueblo ceramic traditions. We can trace the sand used to temper many Salado Polychrome vessels to the general vicinity of Reeve Ruin and Davis Ranch Ruin, indicating that migrant potters and their

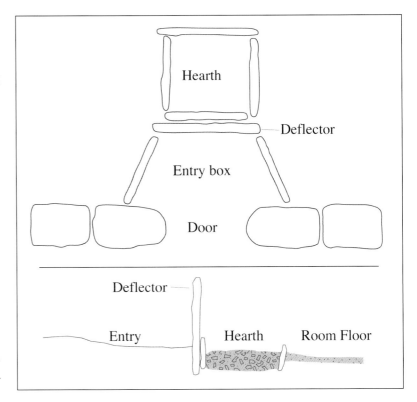

Figure 12.5. A slab-lined entry box, accompanied by a square hearth also lined with stone, is a marker of Kayenta immigrants in the San Pedro Valley. Low slabs on either side of the room's entrance might have trapped blowing sand, and the taller slab in the middle shielded the hearth from wind blowing in the door. *Top:* plan view; *bottom:* cross section.

descendants were the primary producers. Salado Polychrome dominates the ceramics we find at nearly all San Pedro Valley sites throughout the fourteenth century.

The use of obsidian, ideal for making razor-sharp stone tools and weapons, also increased markedly in the northern San Pedro Valley during this interval. Thanks to trace-element analysis, we know that much of this obsidian came from sources near the Safford Basin, which lay along the migration route. Kayenta enclaves in the Cascabel district have considerably more obsidian than do local platform mound villages. The immigrants also controlled the trade of this valuable raw material within the valley, perhaps by staying in touch with relatives who had recently moved to the Safford area. Although small in numbers, Kayenta groups became a powerful minority in the northern San Pedro Valley a generation or two after their arrival.

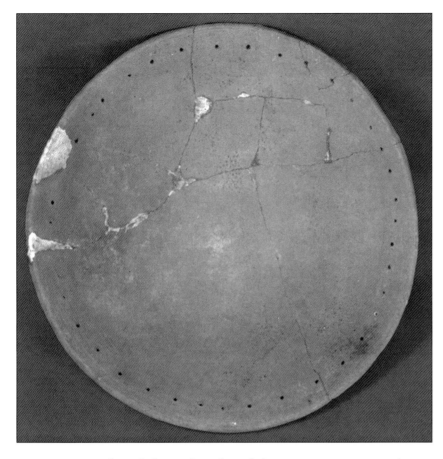

Figure 12.6. A perforated plate in the style made by Kayenta immigrants in the northern San Pedro Valley.

Figure 12.7. A San Carlos Red-on-brown bowl similar to those made by local San Pedro potters.

After several generations of close interaction, the distinctions between immigrants and locals blurred. The last Classic period sites to be built contain complicated mixtures of migrant and local artifacts and architecture, indicating that members of the two groups intermarried and lived in the same settlements. Sites from this period contain decorated pottery, turquoise, and obsidian and have mounded accumulations of melted adobe from residential structures. These settlements contained neither platform mounds nor kivas. This mixing of peoples may have led to the birth of a new collective identity by the late 1300s that included elements of both local and immigrant cultures.

Decline and Disappearance?
Despite this picture of harmony and prosperity, population declined in the northern San Pedro Valley throughout the 1300s. This loss of people suggests that communities were under severe stress. Judging from room counts, approximately 1,500 people lived in the San Pedro Valley during the early fourteenth century. By late in the century, no more than 1,000 people inhabited the valley, and by the early 1400s, the number had dropped below 500.

Although population decline opened up vast tracts of farmland, cultivators continued to live in villages instead of dispersing across the landscape. But however appealing or necessary life in a walled platform mound settlement was in the short term,

Figure 12.8. A Kayenta-style kiva at Davis Ranch Ruin with bench, loom holes, ventilator, and foot drum.

in the long term these villages were unsustainable. Living in close quarters in a hot environment promoted poor sanitation and diseases to which children would have been particularly vulnerable. A relatively small change in the balance between birth and death rates could have accounted for such population decline if it took place gradually over a hundred years. In addition, people would have overused the farmland around the major villages, leading to environmental degradation and smaller harvests.

This decline must have been apparent by 1400 as the remaining people of the San Pedro Valley walked by the ruins of once thriving villages. Nevertheless, these people continued to live in tightly packed settlements as overall numbers in the valley declined. By 1400 only a few settlements remained in the Dudleyville and northern Aravaipa

districts. By 1450 even the last villages were gone. Not a single site has been identified in the northern San Pedro Valley that dates between 1450 and 1650, shortly before Spaniards established permanent settlements in southern Arizona. A few people may have continued to live in the valley, but archaeologists have not identified their settlements. Some families might have moved to the Phoenix Basin, but population was falling there as well. Still others might have traveled the long road back north, to Zuni and the Hopi mesas. I wonder whether those who went back to the Pueblo world were recognized as relatives returning home after a long absence or whether they had been changed so much by their desert sojourn that they were again regarded as foreigners.

During those last years in the fifteenth century, did the final San Pedro villagers sense some external threat present that remains invisible to archaeologists? Were the village residents or their leaders afraid of change during a time of stress, stubbornly clinging to a way of life that no longer worked? These are questions for future archaeologists armed with more data and new analytical techniques.

Jeffery J. Clark is a preservation archaeologist with the Center for Desert Archaeology in Tucson, Arizona. His Hohokam research has emphasized the San Pedro Valley and Tonto Basin, where his primary interests have been migration and cultural identity, spatial analysis, and architectural studies.

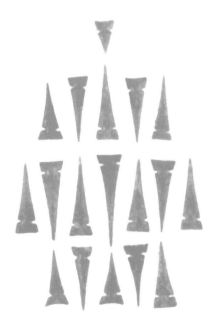

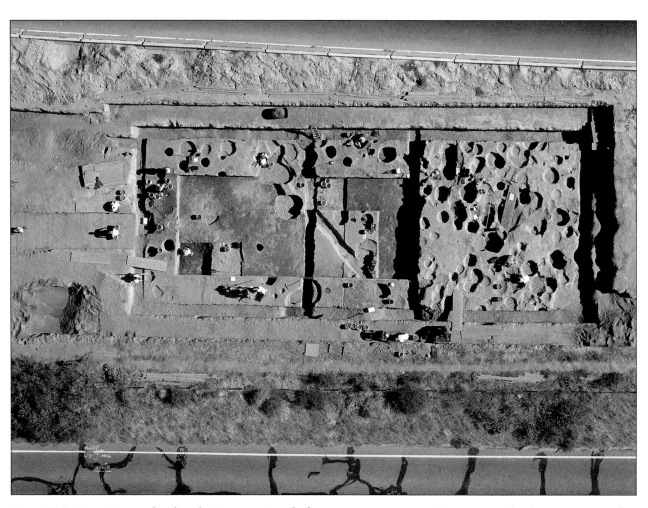

Figure 13.1. Excavations undertaken during expansion of a freeway entrance ramp in Tucson exposed a dramatic pattern of pithouses yielding remains of early corn.

Laws, Dollars, and Scholars
The Business of Hohokam Archaeology

William H. Doelle

I own a for-profit firm that specializes in doing Hohokam archaeology. I spend much of my time dealing with finances because every two weeks I must cover the paychecks of my 35 full-time staff and up to 30 part-time field staff. Hohokam archaeology was not always done this way. The laws that guide my daily work were developed and refined over more than a century, and they have transformed the profession of archaeology. "Following the money" reveals a great deal about the roots of today's Hohokam archaeology because money, laws, and the institutions in which scholars work have a long and dynamic relationship.

In the 1880s wealthy easterner Mary Hemenway selected Frank Cushing, a young scholar of Zuni ethnography, to lead an expedition that resulted in 15 months of excavation in the Salt River valley in 1887–88 (fig. 13.2). Cushing earned $150 (2005 value: $2,940) per month. Phoenix was a tiny town of just over 3,000 people when he excavated some of the most important Hohokam villages dating from the 1200s into the 1400s. Ultimately, the artifacts ended up at Harvard's Peabody Museum, but Cushing's poor health and tensions among the expedition team prevented the publication of their findings. It was an early lesson that big money does not guarantee successful research.

Eastern money sponsored many expeditions throughout the Southwest to build the collections of Eastern museums. As regional populations grew, they became increasingly discontent to see local treasures loaded on east-bound trains. Excavations by a Swede at Mesa Verde in the 1890s galvanized congressional action. In 1906, Congress passed a national Antiquities Act that outlawed looting and implemented a permit process for excavations on federal land. It served notice that the archaeological resources of the United States were part of the national heritage.

Figure 13.2. Frank Hamilton Cushing, the first Hohokam archaeologist and Zuni ethnographer, in about 1882.

Federal dollars flowed at a slow trickle that helped advance Hohokam archaeology in these early years. For example, Cushing and others testified before Congress in 1889 and won an appropriation of $2,000 (2005 value: $41,670) for repair work at Casa Grande Ruin (fig. 13.3). Cosmos and Victor Mindeleff and Jesse Walter Fewkes, from the Smithsonian Institution, did some important work at Casa Grande Ruin, which in 1892 became the first federal archaeological preserve to be established in the United States. Passage of the Antiquities Act triggered the designation of national monuments in southern Arizona at Montezuma's Castle (1906), Tonto Cliff Dwelling (1907), and Casa Grande (1918). But few Hohokam sites have well-preserved architecture, so the government's emphasis on visible prehistoric buildings restricted direct federal ownership to a few unusual Hohokam ruins.

Figure 13.3. A roof protects the adobe "Big House" at Casa Grande National Monument.

In 1924 the eminent archaeologist Alfred Vincent Kidder published a masterful synthesis of Southwestern archaeology. That same year, his cousin arranged a family camping trip to the Southwest. Serendipitously, a wealthy Californian named Harold S. Gladwin was invited along. Under Kidder's tutelage, Gladwin discovered a new passion. A man of action, he accepted Kidder's challenge to explore the "Red-on-buff Culture"—named for its characteristic buff-colored pottery with red paint—of southern Arizona.

Gladwin moved to Globe, Arizona, built a research institution called Gila Pueblo, and commissioned very large-scale surveys to define the boundaries of this poorly known archaeological culture. In 1930 he cut a deal with a promising young archaeologist named Emil W. Haury. He would pay Haury for two years to earn a PhD at Harvard, and Haury would work for him during the summers and for three years after he received his degree. Haury's pay rate was $150 (2005 value: $2,240) per month while at Harvard and $300 per month in Arizona. Before heading to Harvard, Haury excavated a site on the south side of Lake Roosevelt. His report began the formal definition of the Hohokam culture. Haury's Harvard dissertation was an analysis of the artifacts from the Hemenway expedition led by Cushing. After graduation, Haury joined Gladwin for excavations in 1935 and 1936 at Snaketown, a large site on the Gila River (figs. 13.4, 13.5). Their work was funded mostly by Gladwin's personal resources.

Meanwhile, Byron Cummings came to Arizona from Utah in 1915 and became the first director of the Arizona State Museum at the University of Arizona. A champion of Arizona's rich prehistory, he was instrumental in getting state support for archaeology and passage of a state Antiquities Act in 1927. As with the federal Antiquities Act of 1906, the motivation was a desire to keep Arizona's archaeological collections within the state rather than in the vaults of Eastern museums. Its passage reflected the emergence of local institutions for archaeological research. Only much later, in 1960, was a more comprehensive state act passed, under the guidance of Emil Haury.

In 1937 Haury left Gila Pueblo to chair the University of Arizona's Department of Archaeology (soon to become the Department of Anthropology); later he took Cummings's place as director of the Arizona State Museum. He quickly initiated the Papagueria Project with Works Progress Administration (WPA) funding, and two master's degree students excavated sites in the eastern portion of what is now the Tohono O'odham Reservation.

Figure 13.4. Excavations at Snaketown in 1935–36.

Figure 13.5. Participants in the 1935–36 Snaketown excavation. *Left to right:* Emil Haury, Julian Hayden, Evelyn Dennis, Irwin Hayden, E. B. Sayles, Nancy Pinkley, Erik Reed, and Fisher Motz.

Farther west on the reservation, Julian Hayden directed fieldwork at the deeply stratified site of Ventana Cave. Although these projects failed to resolve research questions about the transition from pre-Hispanic to postcontact times, they led Haury to divide the Hohokam into a River Branch and a Desert Branch. Then the United States entered World War II, and Hohokam archaeology went largely dormant for the next two decades.

New forms of government funding gradually brought Hohokam archaeology back to life. The practice of "salvage" archaeology had emerged first in Egypt in 1907, when government officials responded to the destruction of the country's heritage caused by construction of the original Aswan Dam. In the United States, "reservoir salvage" excavations accompanied massive dam construction programs such as those of the Tennessee Valley

Authority in the 1930s. In the early 1950s, "highway salvage" archaeology appeared, first in New Mexico and then in Arizona. These early developments fostered the regulation-driven work today called "cultural resource management," or CRM.

At the Arizona State Museum, William Wasley directed the early Highway Salvage Program, beginning in 1955. His work at Painted Rocks Reservoir, around Gila Bend, Arizona, highlights an intellectual conundrum that differentiates academic from CRM archaeologists. Academic archaeologists do their best to select the places they investigate to best answer their research questions, whereas CRM

Figure 13.6. Snaketown excavations with a backhoe in the 1960s.

archaeologists do research wherever a destructive activity such as road building or commercial development is about to take place. They must assess the situation and formulate research questions appropriate to the archaeological resources at hand. Wasley faced the effects of a large new reservoir. He and his assistant, Al Johnson, excavated at major ball court villages, but they ignored smaller sites that were even more directly threatened. These small sites may have been the remains of groups from the Lower Colorado River who moved into the Hohokam area, an important research topic that remains poorly understood even today. Not only did Wasley and Johnson consciously decided to apply their limited budget to the larger ball court sites, but they also won a grant of $13,700 (2005 value: $86,160) from the National Science Foundation to excavate a dramatic hilltop ruin—a site that the reservoir did not threaten in the least.

At about the same time, the National Science Foundation awarded a particularly important grant to Emil Haury—$115,600 (2005 value: $727,000) for a restudy of Snaketown. Salvage work was making it increasingly apparent that debates and uncertainties about Hohokam chronology required new information. Haury believed that revisiting Snaketown could best supply that information, and he under-

took a major excavation there in 1964–65 (fig. 13.6).

New laws, particularly the National Historic Preservation Act of 1966 and the National Environmental Policy Act of 1970, soon changed the way archaeology was done. Archaeological assessment, ideally done early in the planning stages, became a legal requirement for development projects. Occasionally, such assessments can lead to decisions to preserve sites, but more often excavators obtain samples of site information before construction goes forward and destroys the last remnants. Under the new laws, the demand for archaeological projects burgeoned. It was met initially by university- and museum-based institutions in Arizona, but between the mid-1970s and 1990, new, private-sector firms largely took over this contract-funded work. Today private-sector archaeology in the United States brings in more than a quarter of a billion dollars per year, and Arizona's firms do at least $15 million in business annually.

I did not begin my career, however, working for a private firm. To pay my way through graduate school, I took a summer job at the Arizona State Museum in 1974. At a pay rate of $1.70 (2005 value: $6.75) per hour, I delved into Hohokam archaeology, initiated my career in CRM, and experienced the rapid changes in both areas. In this first job, I was responsible for writing a research plan for a large archaeological survey along the Gila River. I had never worked in the Hohokam area, but it took only a few weeks to read all the published literature then available. It was still two years before the publication of Emil Haury's report on his 1964-65 excavations at Snaketown, but other archaeologists were exploring exciting new directions in Hohokam research. David Doyel was supervising excavations at the Classic period platform mound community of Escalante on the Gila River. Arizona State University graduate students Mark Raab and Al Goodyear were using surface survey and environmental data to better understand past Hohokam subsistence practices and settlement patterns. At the national level, Bill Lipe was developing a new conservation model for American archaeology. Calling for more active preservation on a large scale, Lipe highlighted the fact that archaeological resources are nonrenewable and should be "consumed" with caution.

Change was in the air at the Arizona State Museum in those days. I worked for the recently established Cultural Resource Management Division. The separate Highway Salvage Program hit its peak size of six full-time employees in 1974–75. After that, the Department of Transportation imposed severe cutbacks, and the Museum's CRM Division managed the salvage program in its final three years. The CRM Division grew gradually throughout the late 1970s and then took off in 1979 in response to the Salt-Gila Aqueduct Project, the first "mega-project" in southern Arizona. Salt-Gila represented one of the three major segments in the US Bureau of Reclamation's Central Arizona Project, the creation of a massive artificial river in which water flows uphill from the Colorado River to Phoenix and then south to Tucson.

The Salt-Gila Aqueduct Project had a budget over $1.7 million (2005 value: $4.57 million), about six times larger than Haury's Snaketown project 15 years earlier. It involved fieldwork at 45 sites along a 58-mile corridor across the southern Arizona desert south of Phoenix. Salt-Gila crews did a lot of digging—some 70 person-years worth —and produced huge quantities of data in a very short time, much more than anyone had been accustomed to dealing with. Although the Salt-Gila project produced important substantive results, it was the ways in which team members gathered, organized, reported, and interpreted data that most transformed the practice of Hohokam archaeology.

The contrast between the approach taken to writing up the results of the Salt-Gila Project and Emil Haury's approach at Snaketown is stark. Haury nearly single-handedly shouldered the burden of compiling and interpreting the findings from his substantial excavations. He wrote every single chapter of the 357-page final report, from the environmental background to the excavation description and chapters on all types of artifacts. In contrast, the researchers working on the Salt-Gila Project produced altogether 16 volumes of reports reaching a page total of just over 3,900. Project members published their research design and descriptions of all the excavated sites. They reported on the artifacts found and the environmental samples in separate volumes, and the final volume provided synthesis and conclusions. To publish his book took Haury a full decade after his fieldwork ended, whereas the entire Salt-Gila Project lasted only six years from start to finished reports.

With its grand scale, the Salt-Gila field effort played a dramatic role as a training ground. Archaeologists are generally trained at field schools held by universities during the summers. But scorching summers had stymied formal training of this sort in Hohokam archaeology, together with work in many of southern Arizona's environmental zones. As a result, on-the-job learning was a critical element for Salt-Gila success but a daunting prospect for a project with 300 people on its personnel list. It is notable that three dozen of those staff members are now active professionals with either *MA* or *PhD* after their names. The Salt-Gila Project helped train a large percentage of the Hohokam archaeologists who have made a difference during the past quarter-century.

While the Salt-Gila Project was gearing up, Paul Fish and Suzanne Fish began a unique project through the Arizona State Museum. Their Northern Tucson Basin Project involved an intensive regional survey of more than 900 square miles. They funded their research and the training of university students with money from the Bureau of Reclamation for archaeological work farther south along the Central Arizona Aqueduct and from several state sources. They also won National Science Founda-tion grants to conduct excavations at sites of the prehistoric Marana Community. These researchers even came up with a creative solution to the problem of holding field schools in the desert. They incorporated the fieldwork into University of Arizona classes during the fall and spring semesters, avoiding the worst of the summer heat. The Tucson Basin work led to productive models of Hohokam community organization and the preservation of some important sites.

As CRM increasingly offered opportunities for funding, Arizona State University built up its contract-funded program during the 1970s, as did the Museum of Northern Arizona. When the Highway Salvage Program at the Arizona State Museum closed, the Arizona Department of Transportation began using a competitive bid process when it needed CRM work done. One early, large project in the Phoenix area, the Papago Freeway Project, involved separate contracts with Arizona State University and the Arizona State Museum. (Institutional rivalries generally stimulated better performance.) The Department of Transportation set a high standard by funding background studies that augmented what could be learned by studying narrow highway rights-of-way. In the Papago Freeway Project, to better understand developments at sites along the highway route, specialists used tree-ring data to reconstruct the magnitude of annual stream flows in the ancient Salt River. Evidence of very heavy stream flows just after the 1350s led to models of the collapse of the Salt River Hohokam because of severe flooding.

After the Salt-Gila Project ended in the mid-1980s, the "big three"—the Arizona State Museum, Arizona State University, and the Museum of Northern Arizona—completed the other segments of the Bureau of Reclamation's Central Arizona Project. At the same time, a new trend, the emergence of private CRM firms, was picking up steam. In the mid-1970s Lyle Stone had moved to Arizona as a solo consultant. In 1977 three Arizona State University graduate students founded Arizona

Consulting Services, and Larry Hammack left the Arizona State Museum's Highway Salvage Program to start a private firm. Many other companies were launched in the early 1980s. Firms started small and grew to have archaeological staffs of 20, 30, or more. Two developments were key to the privatizing going on in Arizona archaeology. First, Raymond Thompson, director of the Arizona State Museum, effected a change in the state Antiquities Act that allowed the state to issue permits to for-profit firms. Second, museums began to offer curation services so that the new companies had a legitimate place in which to deposit, "in perpetuity," the artifact collections, photographs, and paper records that their work produced.

My own firm started very small in 1982. I opened an Arizona division for a California-based nonprofit, and my first competitive bid was successful. I had been drawing unemployment, as had my pregnant wife, because our previous jobs had ended with the cancellation of a major government project. I remember the relief and satisfaction I felt when I held my first paycheck—my pay rate was $12.50 (2005 value: $25.30) per hour—and gradually I gained confidence that for-profit archaeology could be a viable way to earn a living. In 1989 I was able to buy the Arizona assets of the California-based parent company for $131,000 (2005 value: $206,300) and became truly independent as a new for-profit firm, Desert Archaeology, Inc. Over the years my staff has completed diverse, intellectually stimulating projects that have led to important research advances. My work is now largely administrative. One of the most productive of our recent projects took place right along Interstate 10 through Tucson.

Archaeologists have long wanted to understand better when and how maize, the foundation of the major prehistoric cultures of the Southwest, entered the region from Mesoamerica. Our opportunity to address these questions began with a competitive bid. The Arizona Department of Transportation selected us as the contractor for multiple projects as part of an effort to upgrade Tucson frontage roads for Interstate 10. The target area promised little on the surface. We were about to excavate former plowed fields, amid the noise and fumes

Figure 13.7. Archaeologist Jonathan Mabry indicates the cross section of a 3,000-year-old canal along the Santa Cruz River in Tucson.

of the highway and the railroad, near two sewage treatment plants. How could anything be left?

Despite unpromising appearances, peeling away those surface layers revealed a dramatic pattern. We found hundreds of small, circular pithouses that yielded radiocarbon dates for maize fragments of between 2,000 and 3,000 years ago. These dates were well within the known range of maize cultivation in the Southwest, but the scale of the settlements was a complete surprise. Subsequent work wedged between an on-ramp and a frontage road revealed irrigation canals that were 3,000 years old (fig. 13.7). In the freeway median we discovered the preserved planting holes of a 3,000-year-old maize field. Still other, related projects now place the arrival of maize in southern Arizona around 4,000 years ago and the practice of irrigation at least 3,500 years ago. These may not be the final answers, but it has been astounding to observe the pace of change in our understanding of the region's agricultural foundations.

With the founding of the nonprofit Center for Desert Archaeology, I have been working to bring more private-sector funding into Hohokam research. In late 1997 the center received an endowment gift of $1.8 million (2005 value: $2.19 million), and we have used National Science Foundation and private

foundation grants for studies in the San Pedro Valley (see chapter 12). Research using archaeological collections in museums is the focus of another National Science Foundation grant for comparing the San Pedro Valley with four other areas. Exploring sites on a large spatial scale, using new technologies to better understand existing collections, and integrating old and new field research hold great promise for answering some enduring questions about the Hohokam. The Center for Desert Archaeology also works to preserve sites through ownership or the holding of conservation easements.

In the 1880s there were no regulations to structure Cushing's privately funded fieldwork at large Hohokam sites. Today a complex set of laws mandates archaeological surveys and excavations prior to development projects. An entire new private-sector profession, cultural resource management, has grown up and is the career choice of several hundred archaeologists in Arizona. CRM helps offset the destruction of cultural resources valued by archaeologists, the general public, and modern Native American communities. Nevertheless, the loss of archaeological sites to population growth and urban sprawl in the Hohokam region is overwhelming. The term *Hohokam* derives from the word *huhugam*, which in the O'odham language is often translated as "all used up." Ironically, the development that is fueling the dramatic new insights chronicled in this book may soon leave us a Hohokam archaeology that is indeed *huhugam*.

William H. Doelle is president of Desert Archaeology, Inc., and president and CEO of the nonprofit Center for Desert Archaeology. The Hohokam figure prominently in his combined studies in ethnohistory, archaeological demography, and public archaeology. He is known for promoting innovative research within legally required investigations.

Figure 14.1. A Tohono O'odham saguaro camp in the 1940s, near Ventana Cave.

fourteen

Huhugam

Daniel Lopez

Nac wuḍ Huhugam ha-amjiḍkam 'acim O'odham? Bac 'amjiḍ hihim 'a:cim Tohono O'odham? No 'a wo'o mac wuḍ ha-amjiḍkam hegam mac hab ha-a'aga Huhugam?

Ha'icu t-a:gida 'amjiḍ 'ac s-ma:c g hekĭ hu t-himdag. Am ha'icu t-a:gida 'eḍ 'o 'am 'a:gas 'ab ha-amjiḍ hegam maṣ wuḍ wu: ṣkam matṣ ab i-wu:ha jeweḍ weco amjiḍ k ab i-ha-we:mt hegam maṣ in ki: jeweḍ da:m k ha-ceggia hegam ñuwĭ c hegam maṣ ab si wemaj. Matṣ am 'i-ha-oid k gm hu ha-a'ahe Siwañ Wa'a Ki: c-eḍ k 'am ha-ceggia.

Ñeid an g Siwañ Wa'a Ki: kc amjiḍ ha'icu s-ma:c.
Mac am I-ha-u'u g a'al c am ha-ce:gid g Siwañ Wa'a Ki k amjiḍ s-ma:c mo in cem ha'icugkahim hegam mac hab ha-a'aga Huhugam.
B-o cece g kekelbaḍ mac g Huhugam ha-amjiḍ hihim c in hab ha'icug hemu.

Ñeid an g Wiñta:na Ce:ho kc amjiḍ s-ma:c mo in ha'icugkahim hegam mac hab ha-a'aga Huhugam.
Ñeid an g na:nko ha'icu mat ab 'i-e-wu:has 'ab amjiḍ hegai ce:ho mo hemu ab we:c Cuk Ṣon Kekal Ha-maṣcamakuḍ ab. Na:nko ha'icu mac 'a:cim am hejel tu'akc mo wuḍ si hekĭ hu ha'icu 'ac amjiḍ s-ma:c mo in ha'icugkahim g Huhugam.

Mu'icc 'ac ñeid g hohodai t-ab ha'icu o'ohona kc 'amjiḍ s-ma:c mo in ha'icugkahim g Huhugam.
Pi 'ac ma:c has wuḍ 'a'aga g ha-o'ohona kc 'aṣaba s-ma:c mo wuḍ Huhugam ha'icu ha-a:gida.

Ñeid 'añ g A'al Hiha'iñ mañ hekid 'am ha'icu 'iagculit. Pi 'ac heḍai s-ma:c mas he'ekkia 'i 'a'ahidag 'ab 'am hab cu'ig 'i:da hiha'iñ. Bañ 'elid mo 'ab Huhugam O'odham ha-

amjiḍ hab cu'ig 'i:da hiha'iñ.
Ñeid 'añ g I'itoi Ki: mo ṣa'i si mu'i 'a'ahidag 'amjiḍ 'ab hab cu'ig.

Hegam hohodai koklhai mo 'am hab cu'ig do:da'ag da:m o am ep t-ce:gid mo an cem ki:kahim g Huhugam. Idam hohodai koklhai o mu'l 'a'ahidag ab an hab cu'igkahim mat an cem daḍaiwup hegam hemajkam c amjiḍ ha'icu ñeid. Mu'ij o idam sikolk koklhai matp wuḍcem Huhugam ha-ki:dag.

Am ha'icu t-a:gida 'eḍ 'o 'am 'a:gas mo hekid ha'icu ha-kuḍut g O'odham kut 'ab 'o ñei g I'itoi 'ab ki:j 'ab k-ab 'o tai g 'i-we:mta. Ha'icu t-a:gida 'o 'am t-taṣogid mac hekĭ hua'l 'amjiḍ 'in ha'icug 'a:cim O'odham.

S-ma:c ac mañ hebai amjiḍ him!
S-ma:c ac a:cim O'odham mac hebai amjiḍ hihim c in hab ha'icug hemu. Bo cece g kekelbaḍ mac 'a:cim O'odham 'ab ha-amjiḍ hihim g Huhugam.

S-ma:c 'ac mac 'ab ha-ab gi'i g Huhugam 'ab 'amjiḍ hegai na:nko ha'icu mo 'in hab cu'ig t-jeweḍga da:m. S-ma:c 'ac mac 'ab ha-amjiḍ hihim hegam hekĭ hi O'odham mac hemu hab ha-a'aga Huhugam.

I:da jewed mac 'in da:m 'oyopo 'ac s-ma:c mo wuḍ Huhugam ha-ki:dag 'i:da jewed mac 'in da:m ki:dag hemu. Ta:tk 'ac g Huhugam ha-gewkdag mo we:sko ha'icug 'an t-we:gaj. Mo ha'icug g ha-gewkdag do:da'ag ceḍ c 'an ha'icug g he-gewkdag jeweḍ da:m c 'an ha'icug g ha-gewkdag hewel ceḍ.

Figure 14.2. Danny Lopez, Tohono O'odham tribal elder, cultural preservationist, and educator.

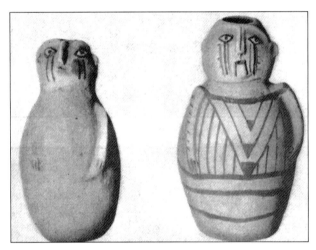

Figure 14.3. Akimel O'odham (Pima) effigy vessels from the early 1900s show continuity with Hohokam pottery traditions. Compare with plates 3 and 4.

Huhugam

The O'odham elders used to say that the Huhugam were a people who lived a very long time ago. Our elders of the past did not know the time when these people lived here. The elders simply talked of them as long-ago people or those that are gone. Even though they did not really know much about them, our elders still said that the Huhugam were our ancestors (figs. 14.2, 14.3).

The word *huhugam* means "something that is all gone," such as food or when something disappears. *Huhugam* is used to refer to those people who have disappeared.

Who really knows who they were or what happened to them? Did they really all die off, as some theories say, or did all or some of them remain to be the forefathers of the modern-day Tohono O'odham?

Today we are here, the Tohono O'odham, and we do not know how far our past generations go back in time. We just say that we go back to the Huhugam. We are here today, but we know that some time in the future we will also be called the Huhugam.

There are certain places on Tohono O'odham land and in what is now Sonora that remind modern O'odham of our ancient ancestors that we call the Huhugam. Some sites are well-known places that have been documented by anthropologists, but there are other places that are not so well known, even by tribal people. Because of recent intrusion by photographers and writers, certain sites have been closed off to tourists.

The Children's Shrine is an ancient site that, according to tribal legends, is the place where four children were offered to the water to avoid a flood.

Figure 14.4. Excavation of Ventana Cave in the 1940s.

saw the shrine many years later, I was moved as I prayed and made my offering.

I'itoi Ki is the other well-known sacred shrine. According to tribal legends, the cave is the place where I'itoi lived when he was here on earth. According to our legends, I'itoi was the creator of the world and the O'odham. Whenever the Desert People were in great danger, they would summon I'itoi to come and help them. Such was the case with the Eagle Man and Ho'oki Oks, when I'itoi came to destroy these two terrible monsters. Today O'odham still go to the cave to pray and ask I'itoi for help. O'odham know that this cave is very old.

Ho'oki Ki in Sonora reminds us of another one of our ancient legends, which tells of a monster woman who killed little children for her food. As in other stories, I'itoi came to help his people. According to legend, this cave is where Ho'oki was burned to death. Seeing the legendary site seems to make the story come alive. We also go to this place to make offerings and pray because it reminds us of our past.

Ventana Cave is well known by O'odham and non-O'odham as a place that was inhabited by the ancient ones. The Huhugam were there in this part of the world, and because of the excavation of the cave, artifacts show their way of life (fig. 14.4). Our grandfathers used to say that Huhugam lived there and that they were our ancestors.

The Big House, or Siwan Wa'a Ki:, is another site well known to all people and mentioned in O'odham legends. The world knows that Casa Grande Ruin has been there for hundreds of years. O'odham know that the place is ancient because it is mentioned in some of the tribal legends. Siwa

No one really knows when that happened, but O'odham know that this is a very ancient place. Does it date back to the Huhugam? We do not know, but we know that it is a sacred shrine and that the event happened a very long time ago.

As a child I heard about the shrine from my parents and grandparents, but I never saw the sacred place until I was an adult. Every time my mother told me her version of the Children's Shrine account, I was always intrigued and used my imagination to see the story come alive. When I finally

Figure 14.5. Early photograph of the "Big House" at Casa Grande National Monument.

Wa'a Ki: is a place where O'odham can go to pray or sings songs to the Huhugam spirits. The non-O'odham call this sacred place Casa Grande Ruin (fig. 14.5).

The ancient foot trails to the Gulf of Mexico are another reminder to O'odham of our past—the Huhugam. The cave of I'itoi at one of the giant craters in the Pinacate Mountains in Sonora makes that part of the land a historical and legendary place for us.

These places are what we consider sacred places because they are the evidence that reminds us of the long-ago people, or Huhugam. We do not excavate sites and date the artifacts that we have, but we have faith in our elders, in the sacred places, in our stories, and in I'itoi.

The earth gives us a sense of connection to the people of the past. That is why we say that the earth is holy and should not be disturbed, because the land belongs to the spirits. Even in the mountains we can feel the power of the Huhugam spirits as we journey to the mountain villages. As we breathe the holy air that gives us life, we can feel the power of our ancestors. When we see the stars at night and hear the owl, some of us feel strongly that we are a part of the ancient past.

Daniel Lopez is a faculty member at the Tohono O'odham Community College in Sells, Arizona, where he follows his passion for culture and language preservation through that institution's Himdag program. He is from the Big Fields District of the Tohono O'odham Nation and is involved in Tohono O'odham Community Action, a program supporting sustainable community development.

Figure 15.1. Akimel O'odham women carrying a basket of cotton and a jar, as drawn by botanist Arthur Schott in 1854.

O'odham Traditions about the Hohokam

Donald M. Bahr

When Spaniards journeyed to southern Arizona in the seventeenth century, they met the O'odham, native people who spoke the Piman, or O'odham, language. The O'odham lived in a majority of the territory that previously had been home to the Hohokam, but they were not the sole occupants of that land (map 2). Today, as at the time of Spanish contact, they share this territory with speakers of Yuman languages: the Maricopas (Pi:pa:s), who live west of the Phoenix Basin, once the center of the Hohokam world, and the Yavapais (Yavpay), who live to the north (figs. 15.2, 15.3).

Archaeologists, in their study of material culture, generally see the closest resemblances between the Hohokam and the O'odham. But such resemblances go only so far in defining meaningful cultural connections between more recent groups and ancestral peoples. How do these Native Americans perceive their relationship to the Hohokam predecessors? The differing oral traditions of the O'odham, Maricopas, and Yavapais reveal much in this regard. In what follows, I look at the oral histories and stories relevant to Hohokam connections, beginning with those of the O'odham.

Figure 15.2. In an 1846 lithograph by Major W. H. Emory, Akimel O'odham and Maricopas trade with American soldiers.

Figure 15.3. Qua-tha, a Yavapai scout, about 1882.

Figure 15.4. A traditional Akimel O'odham dwelling, about 1938.

Nowadays, two divisions of O'odham live north of the US-Mexico border. The Akimel O'odham, or "River People" (formerly called Pima), live in south-central Arizona, and the Tohono O'odham, or "Desert People" (formerly called Papago), live in southwestern Arizona (fig. 15.1, plate 22). Their shared sense of ancientness does much to make them feel that they are one people. They had a common origin, according to the oral traditions they largely share.

When archaeologists first came to O'odham country and asked who had made the potsherds and mounds there, they probably received the answer, "Huhugam O'odham." The word *huhugam*, which the archaeologists converted into "Hohokam," refers to anything that is finished and no longer exists. Thus, one can say *huhugam o'odham*, meaning "finished people-like-us." The word *o'odham* can also mean "Native American" or "human." To the O'odham, the Ancestral Pueblos and ancient Egyptians are also *huhugam*, as are all ways of life that once were and are no more. Indeed, this ubiquitous word can refer to many things besides people, such as water, cooked food, and money.

In their oral traditions, the O'odham were especially concerned with one "finished people," the Huhugam O'odham, who they believed spoke the same language they did and whom they believed their ancestors had destroyed. The creation, adventures, and destruction of this people take up nearly all of what Euro-Americans might call O'odham mythology and what the O'odham consider to be more a history. They call the whole of this history-mythology the "Ho'ok A:gida," the "Witch Telling," after the name of one important character, a female called "Witch" who lived with and preyed upon the now "finished" people.

The O'odham organized the whole of their "Witch Telling" into a single chronicle. I write this in the past tense because I refer especially to the O'odham storytellers of the 1930s and before. Also, the tellings I refer to come from the Akimel O'odham, who live along the Gila and Salt Rivers in the core area of archaeology's Hohokam culture (fig. 15.4). An expert storyteller would know 30 to 50 distinct stories, of which a few, such as the O'odham story of Witch, figured prominently in the main story line.

The central story line goes like this: At the beginning, a man-god named Earth Medicine-man made the earth, sun, moon, and stars. Then he caused a handful of other gods to come into existence, the principal of them being Elder-brother. Next he made O'odham-speaking humans. Elder-brother is referred to by that name from the start, but he acquires it only by intransigence after a flood, which is the next important event. Elder-brother, Earth Medicine-man, and a few other beings, including a few of the O'odham-speaking people, survive this flood. The people take refuge in the underworld, while the gods survive by floating in boatlike containers. After the flood, Elder-brother demands that he be called "Elder," a title he does not deserve. He creates a second group of O'odham-speaking people, who will later become the "finished-ones," and he causes Earth Medicine-man to flee to the underworld to join his prior creation, the original people.

Many interesting and important events befall Elder-brother and his second group of people, including the Witch affair and the creation of the white race, which is sent away with the expectation that it will return. Elder-brother's people eventually hate and kill him. He comes back to life, flies across the sky, and enters the underworld at the place where the sun sets. There he meets Earth Medicine-man and the people who are the earlier creation. He leads these first people (but not Earth Medicine-man, their creator) to the earth's surface to make war on, defeat, and "finish off" (*hugio*) his own creation, the then-reigning second people, who also speak an O'odham language.

About the last quarter of the chronicle is taken up with battles between the emergent O'odham and the second O'odham group, which they conquer. After the conquest, Elder-brother leaves the victorious first people and enters seclusion at a certain mountain in Tohono—not Akimel—O'odham territory. Earth Medicine-man remains in the underworld. The conquerors disperse to their present desert (Tohono O'odham) and river (Akimel O'odham) locations, and before long the white people return to their area of origin, though we are not told how. In effect, the chronicle ends the night before the return of the whites.

The set of stories does not quite end with Elder-brother's departure, however. After he leaves, a few stories tell of humans who marry and reproduce normally and are preoccupied with Apaches. The atmosphere of the chronicle changes. The creations are finished, the conquest is over, the gods are gone, and the Apaches make it dangerous for O'odham people to go out alone. This was the situation in which Spaniards found the O'odham in the 1600s.

Unlike Euro-American histories, this O'odham chronicle is organized not in years but around the activities of a few important gods. Their careers span nearly the entire O'odham history, making the whole of ancientness seem short—only a few generations. Normal human procreation and marriage take place only near the end of the account, after these gods have ceased to be active in human affairs. Those earliest humans are disconnected from the oral histories and genealogies of the more recent past of the current O'odham. No one telling the stories knows the precise relation between the storied individuals and persons living today. There is good reason for this. If the Hohokam ceased to exist in the fifteenth century, then many generations passed between the last of the "ancient" O'odham and today's people. Except for the most recent forebears, these intervening generations are not remembered.

Distinctiveness and Oral Traditions

The O'odham and their neighbors had different oral traditions, even though some of the same kinds of episodes appear in each. The differences could be seen as disputes, but the disputes are not voiced openly. Nor are they contradictory in the sense that the truth of one requires the falseness of the other. The differences are significant because having a distinct sense of origins made each of these neighboring groups a distinct people; it gave each of them its unique identity.

Despite similarities in some episodes, the oral traditions of the Maricopa and Yavapai neighbors of the O'odham differ substantially on nearly everything that happened in ancient times. The O'odham say that two distinct creations of people spoke the O'odham language and one came to an end in the past. The Maricopas say that there was just one creation of Maricopa speakers, and their history includes no telling of an extinct "finished people." The Yavapais give no creation story of Yavapai speakers at all. They give origins to the O'odham and white people, but not to themselves; there is no moment when the first Yavapai speakers, or tribal ancestors, were created.

The O'odham creation story tells that the two gods, Earth Medicine-man and Elder-brother, came to ground separately from different floating vessels after the flood. When they met, they argued over who landed first. There was no objective way to settle this argument, so when Elder-brother insisted, Earth Medicine-man sank into the ground rather than live with this insufferable god. As he sank, he sang, "Here I sink, and I know all sorts of things."

The Maricopa mythology also begins with a flood and two man-gods floating, in this case, on a log. This event is not the occasion for a second creation of humans as with the O'odham, and the Maricopa man-gods are on the same log, not enclosed in separate vessels. Thus, the Maricopa situation does not give rise to a dispute over who touched ground (and was "reborn") first. Like Elder-brother and Earth Medicine-man, the Maricopa characters are prickly to each other. One urges the other to jump off the log, and the other does so, but the water is so deep that he sinks and is permanently blinded by the plunge into very salty water. In contrast to the Maricopa version, the O'odham telling of the dispute between the man-gods has them waiting for their vessels to land safely, so they could not know who reached land first.

The Maricopa gods amicably create a full set of races, including whites, once they alight. They make people from mud, just like Earth Medicine-man and Elder-brother. The Maricopas differentiate their creation story from that of the O'odham by portraying their man-gods as initially more vicious in the log episode but ultimately more cooperative. In the O'odham version of the log episode, two Coyote brothers float on separate logs, one with eyes open and the other with eyes closed. The first tells the other to open his eyes. The other complies and is blinded by salty foam blown by the wind. These Coyotes in the O'odham story create nothing. They squabble over women, and the elder eventually kills the younger. Thus, what is a central creation account among the Maricopas is a minor episode for the O'odham.

The Maricopas and Yavapais do not have "Hohokam stories," but they do have counterparts to a second story I want to consider, that of Ho'ok, "Witch," for whom the entire O'odham mythology is named. In the O'odham version, Ho'ok's mother is a human woman, the daughter of a widely known Hohokam chief, "Morning Green Chief"

(Si'al Cehedag Siwan). The story includes three generations, but most of the persons are not normal humans. Ho'ok's father is a ball kicked by a human young man, so the procreation is abnormal, and Ho'ok herself is a monstrous female who grows claws as a child and eats nothing but meat. Her ultimate food is the flesh of human children. Therefore, Elder-brother devises a means to kill her. She is put to sleep, roasted, and eaten by the parents and relatives of her victims.

The point of contact between the O'odham chronicle and the Maricopa and Yavapai mythologies is not the witch Ho'ok but her mother, a human woman who gives birth normally following an unusual impregnation. The Maricopa woman gives birth to twin boys after impregnation by a gopher. The Yavapai woman gives birth to a son with two fathers, Cloud and Sun. These happenings are long, important stories in each people's chronicle. I conclude that each of the three peoples found satisfaction in a story of children engendered by exceptional means. In keeping with different tribal identities, each had a different story of that sort.

The O'odham attached their woman to the Hohokam, as the daughter of one of the two best-remembered Hohokam chiefs. Can we believe that there actually were such chiefs? It would be difficult for archaeologists to prove that they existed. We can only note that stories of a woman and her unusual impregnation were widespread in the region, and we should ask why the O'odham formed their version around Hohokam persons while the other peoples did not.

The O'odham and the Hohokam

The main line of O'odham mythology—at least of those Akimel O'odham versions from the Hohokam heartland that are fully recorded—is about two rival gods and their double creation of speakers of the O'odham language; the withdrawal of one of the creator man-gods and the ultimate murder of the other by his own people; the resurrection of that god; and the conquest and "finishing off" of the second people by the first. It is an overall story progression unique to the O'odham among the three peoples we are considering.

Figure 15.5. Widespread use of horses, as illustrated by this mounted family photographed around 1900, increased Apache mobility and conflict with neighboring groups.

In a segment found solely in the O'odham chronicle, a well-known story makes a transition from Hohokam conquest to Apache wars (fig. 15.5) within three generations—actually within about 30 years. In the first generation, the O'odham attack and kill a Hohokam chief named Black Sinew-having Chief (S-cuk Tataikam Siwan). Knowing that he will die (the invaders never lose a battle), the chief tells his son to hide as the chief fights his last, to sneak up to him and inhale his final breath, and then to surrender to the invaders. The son follows these instructions, an invading chief adopts him, and the boy marries the chief's daughter, who becomes pregnant. The young hus-

band then goes hunting and is killed by Apaches. The child is raised to become a great warrior against the Apaches. From this story comes an oration that the Akimel and some Tohono O'odham used in their wars with Apaches. Although the transition from the conquest of the Hohokam to the time of Apache conflicts is swift in this account, the story bridges the gap between the last of the Hohokam and the succeeding O'odham with intermarriage and procreation. The child of this union unites with the other O'odham for victory against the Apaches.

The O'odham, Maricopas, and Yavapais each had a mythology with its own characters and themes, each a private album of ancientness that distinguished these neighbors from one another. It is possible that the O'odham stressed the Hohokam because they did indeed grow out of and conquer them in an O'odham-against-O'odham war. It is also possible that the other peoples are silent on the Hohokam not so much because their ancestors did not participate to some extent in that culture but because of deference to, or as a distinction from, the O'odham claims.

Since the eighteenth century, the O'odham, Maricopas, and Yavapais have all lived on land formerly inhabited by archaeology's Hohokam. On the basis of their recorded oral traditions, neither the Maricopas nor the Yavapais told stories of a "finished people" similar to themselves who left ruins and potsherds behind. It seems that local ruins and remains are less meaningful to those peoples than to the O'odham. The O'odham make more of archaeology's Hohokam, and these episodes in their traditions offer potential points of convergence with archaeology's findings, even though much in the O'odham accounts is of a miraculous nature. As a model of such convergence, we know that there is an appreciable body of biblical archaeology, even though it does not touch directly on many of the Bible's miracles. I think that there could be a Ho'ok A:gida archaeology in the future, and I hope that there will be.

Donald M. Bahr, a retired professor of anthropology at Arizona State University, has been a student of O'odham language, culture, social history, and oral tradition for more than 40 years. His book *The Hohokam Chronicles: The Short, Swift Time of Gods on Earth* brings Akimel O'odham oral tradition directly to bear on Pima understandings of the Hohokam.

Figure 16.1. Zig-Zag Mountain in the Santan Range, Gila River Indian Community.

Songscapes and Calendar Sticks

J. Andrew Darling and Barnaby V. Lewis

When was the last time you broke into song? Which song did you sing? Here is an O'odham song about a mountain that stands west of an old Indian trail. Nameless on maps, it is a monument of volcanic and metamorphic rock that is well known in O'odham country:

> Zigzag Connected,
> On top I pause.
> Here beside me,
> Black cloud floats zigzags,
> Pleasant for watching.

Or so says a translation by the anthropologist Donald Bahr. It and translations of other songs in this chapter are drawn from the 1997 book *Ants and Orioles: Showing the Art of Pima Poetry*.

The late Vincent Joseph, an O'odham elder who recorded the song in the 1980s, offered his interpretation: "The Oriole bird, the traveler, while resting on top of Zig-Zag Mountain, sees a black cloud floating below. The cloud imitates the zigzag shape of the mountain, and the Oriole is pleased with what he sees."

Twenty years later, Barnaby Lewis shared the same song as we traveled along a historic O'odham trail on land belonging to the Gila River Indian Community. The morning was not unusual. Our jobs for the Tribe had brought us to inspect recent vandalism to rock art sites on the reservation's northern boundary in the Santan Mountains. From the west, Zig-Zag Mountain stood out clearly (fig. 16.1). Barnaby's singing blessed the moment and honored the spirit of the mountain, even through the windshield of a tribal vehicle.

This chapter is about the way in which descendants of the Huhugam (Hohokam) interpret geographical space through song traditions. We examine songscapes—landscapes remembered through O'odham song—and their relationship to traditional infrastructure for travel and the archaeology of ancient trails. We also consider the dimension of *time*. Time is important for understanding how landscapes, particularly sacred landscapes, exist alongside history. If we wish to appreciate the traditional O'odham's spatial concepts, then we must consider them in the context of O'odham ideas of time and history, specifically the histories told through O'odham calendar sticks.

Trails

Trails are a major part of traditional infrastructure (fig. 16.2). The arid Southwest offers a unique cultural landscape in which trail segments remain visible for a long time on the desert surface. Some are as old as 10,000 years. The products of regular foot travel, desert trails appear as scars in the natural desert pavement, unlike roads or engineered constructions. Native infrastructure includes both the facilities, such as trails, and the ideas that enable communities to function. Knowledge of trails in the past—not just of where people were but how they got there—is important for archaeologists' understanding of the locations and distribution of sacred sites and settlements.

For the O'odham of central and southern Arizona, traveling means more than going from one place to another. Travel is not random. Traditionally, a person can travel on foot and through dreaming.

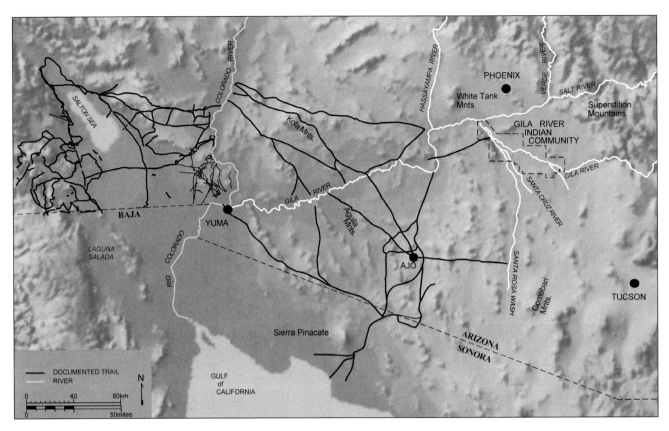

Figure 16.2. Major Native American trail networks in the southern US Southwest and adjacent northwestern Mexico.

An individual acquires songs and spiritual power through dream journeys to spiritual places. Such journeys recapitulate physical travel over the ground and underlie the relationship between beliefs about travel and the actual trails that certain songs or song series represent. In the physical world, journeys must be enacted with geographical precision and spiritual propriety, vital components in surviving desert travel. The same is true for singing songs: They must be sung in the correct order. The repeated performance of O'odham songs expresses and reinforces the experience of travel and the qualities of places in the O'odham world. In this way, the O'odham may know a place through their song culture without having traveled there. In a world without maps, a person who knows the songs is a person who knows where he or she is going. More importantly, a person who knows the songs knows the dangers along the way.

O'odham Social Singing
O'odham social songs, such as the Oriole, Swallow, and Ant songs, accompany traditional dances held

at all-night social events called sings. Whether sacred or secular, songs are never created by singers. Instead, the animal spirits, often birds, compose them and often teach the songs to a singer through dreams. Once a singer has learned a song from an animal spirit, he or she can pass it to other singers through performance and imitation. Songs are typically short and are arranged in an ordered series consisting of as many as 100 individual songs.

Many of these songs have to do with places. One song from the Oriole series, for example, describes the Oriole bird's unsuccessful attempt to enter the mountain known as Crooked Red (fig. 16.3):

> Red Bent, Red Bent.
> Inside songs sound,
> And I am poor [sad],
> I circle behind, Oh, what can I do?
> Now, enter, and then, many songs know.

Often a portion of a particular song series describes a journey, each song representing a place along the way. The geographical aspects of sings

Figure 16.3. Faces on Crooked Red Mountain, Gila River Indian Community. Mountain spirits reveal themselves to remind onlookers of their presence.

and their relationship to archaeological features, especially trails, interest us most here. Donald Bahr observed in *Ants and Orioles*: "It is well to think of social dance song sequences as postcards sent from someone on an impassioned journey. On receiving the card one speculates about the mood of the sender, about all that was happening at the moment of the message… and what the next step in the journey might be."

In a song series, geographical references to place follow a linear, circular, or meandering path without repeated returns to the same location. The sequence of songs creates the geographical itinerary of a particular sing. The Oriole songs serve as a particularly good example that can be tied to the archaeology of ancient trail systems.

Oriole Song Archaeology

The Oriole song series as rendered by Vincent Joseph consists of 47 songs. Fourteen of them, songs 9–22, describe a journey to the salt flats on the Sonoran Gulf Coast. As shown in figure 16.4, the songs describe a circuitous route along which the traveler visits sacred mountains and hot springs. When archaeologists look for evidence that prehistoric people took a long journey similar to this, they

find traces of ancient trails leading from the Gila River Indian Community to the Gulf of California, covering a distance of approximately 286 miles. These trails link the places named in the Oriole songs. Consequently, we can relate specific trails found during archaeological surveys to the itinerary described in the song series.

The westward journey begins by heading north, starting at Blackwater Lake in the Gila River Indian Community and continuing to the Santan Mountains on the reservation's northern boundary. There the songs describe several mountains: White Pinched, Zig-Zag, Crooked Red, and Long Gray. Archaeologists have successfully identified several trails in the mountains, and just as the song sequence directs, they head northeast toward the next destination, the Superstition Mountains. Archaeologists have not traced the trail past the Santans, but the Superstitions are easy to identify and offer the traveler a clear point of orientation.

What do these old trails look like? It depends on local conditions, but intact trails are normally 12 to 20 inches wide. Where they cross desert pavement, they become a clear track or multiple parallel tracks worn as much as two inches below the surface (fig. 16.5). As the trail rises into the Santan

Mountains, it is sometimes deeply incised and shows signs that someone purposefully removed and stacked rocks to clear the way. We also find artifacts, mostly fragments of pottery jars—clear evidence that the Huhugam ancestors of the O'odham used these trails centuries ago, between about 950 and 1450 CE.

After leaving the Superstition Mountains, the Oriole song itinerary proceeds westward through a series of mountain destinations: Iron Mountain, Thin Mountain, and finally, turning south, South Mountain. Archaeologists find scant evidence of a trail connecting these places until they reach the westernmost ridges of South Mountain. According to the Oriole songs, from there the trail crosses the Gila River to a

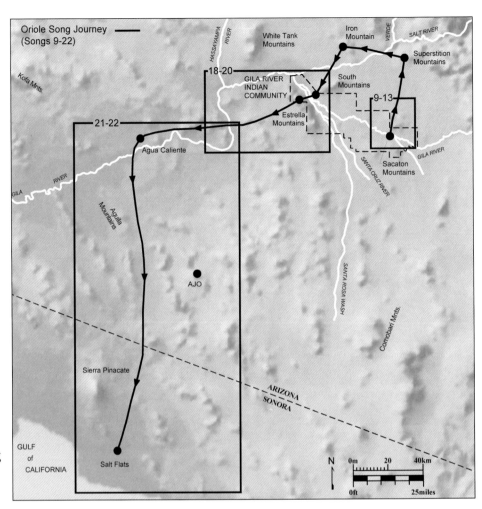

Figure 16.4. The Oriole song itinerary as shared by Vincent Joseph.

place on the west side of the valley. At that point, visible trails head west through a pass in the Estrella Mountains. All along this part of the journey, we find rock art and trail shrines.

On the eastern side of the Estrella Mountains, across a high pass and for a distance of about 22 miles, we find archaeological evidence of a major trail to the west crossing the Rainbow Valley into a pass in the North Maricopa Mountains. It effectively crosscuts the large S-curve in the Gila River. The Spanish missionary Father Kino traveled this part of the trail once in the winter of 1699, but it would have been a difficult route for Europeans burdened by draft animals and equipment.

Field identification of portions of the trail in the Estrella Mountains, the Maricopa Mountains, and the Gila Bend Mountains confirms what the songs

tell us—that this route stretched from the central Hohokam region in the Phoenix Basin to the western periphery of the Hohokam culture area. During the historic period, the trail linked O'odham territory with Yuman (Patayan) areas along the river, places where the Cocamaricopas, Opas (including O'odham and Opas living in mixed villages in the Gila Bend), and Maricopas lived. West of the Maricopa Mountains the trails have survived better than elsewhere, so we can see where the main trail, known as the Komatke Trail (fig. 16.5), split into numerous smaller trails going to villages scattered along the Gila River valley.

Just as rock art and shrines appear along the trails through the Santan Mountains, so we find them here, too, along with fragments of broken pots. Where the Komatke Trail enters the valley of the Gila Bend, archaeologists have found shell arti-

Figure 16.5. A portion of the Komatke Trail heading through the north Maricopa Mountains.

facts, including an unmodified *Glycymeris* shell. The presence of these shells, so prized among the Hohokam for making bracelets, indicates that people traveled and traded goods from the Gulf of California all the way to the middle of the Gila River drainage and beyond.

In the first part of the song journey, 20 songs detail the steps from Blackwater, on the Gila River reservation, to the Estrella Mountains—some 95 miles. Only two songs then carry us to the end of the journey, first to a cluster of hot springs, which some researchers identify as those at Aguacaliente, west of Gila Bend, and finally to the salt flats on the Sonoran coast.

The Tohono O'odham of southwestern Arizona traveled to this shore to gather salt. Along the northern beaches of the Gulf of California, high tides leave salt deposits in a largely uninhabited and waterless landscape. In summer, the Tohono O'odham made pilgrimages to the salt beds, following trails across the desert that connected the few hidden natural tanks holding rainwater.

Salt pilgrimages were significant religious events. Young men and older, experienced male leaders made the arduous journey, which in times past presented some of the same hardships and dangers as going to war. Salt pilgrimages also offered opportunities for dreaming and acquiring spiritual power. Once a man volunteered for his first salt journey, he was committed to three additional trips in successive years, and at the end of each trip he was purified as if returning from battle.

The journey described by the Oriole song cycle describes a route unique to the Akimel O'odham (Gila River Pima). This route suggests that they may have practiced their own salt journey, which included travel to the hot springs in Aguacaliente before turning south to the salt flats in Mexico.

Musical Rasps and Calendar Sticks
For Vincent Joseph, the portion of the Oriole songs describing the westward journey ended at the salt flats. But the song series itself continues with many other songs unrelated to the journey.

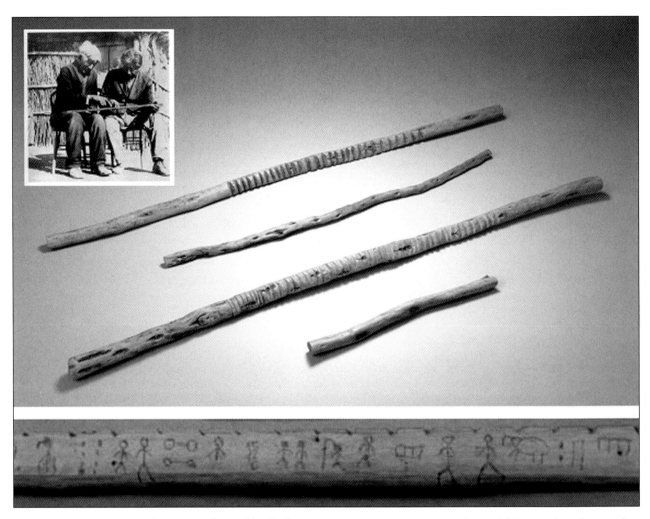

Figure 16.6. *Top:* two sets of rasping sticks used by the late George Kyyitan. *Top inset:* Joseph Head (Maricopa) reading a calendar stick to Henry Soalikee, 1921. *Bottom:* designs (o'ohadag) on a calendar stick.

In Joseph's rendition, the second-to-last song in the series concluded:

> And now we stop singing and scatter.
> Here on our seats our poor scraping sticks lie,
> With song-marks marked where they lie.

Scraping sticks (*hi:ʃkut*) are musical rasps used to accompany traditional singing. They consist of two lengths of greasewood or ironwood, one notched at regular intervals and scraped with the other stick in a rhythm appropriate to the music (fig. 16.6). People also play rasping sticks against a basket or gourd resonator (fig. 16.7). After repeated performances, the spiritual essence of the songs becomes part of the scraping sticks used to perform them. Even when the sticks are no longer used, they retain this spirituality and should be handled respectfully.

Some singers adorn their rasping sticks with carved or painted designs called *o'ohadag*, also known as "song flowers" (*ñe' ñei hiosig*; fig. 16.8). Bahr and his colleagues identify the word for song marks on the sticks as *o'ohon*, meaning "writing," but we feel that *o'ohadag* is more appropriate. *O'ohadag* are representations of the spiritual presence of the songs in these instruments, obtained through their use in performances. The designs are not strictly decorations but are emblematic of the singers' spiritual accomplishment, particularly the song journey. As the Oriole song suggests, song marks appear on the rasping sticks only when the performance is completed.

O'ohadag appear in many other places as well.

Figure 16.7. The Akimel O'odham musician Sides plays a rasping stick on a basket, 1919.

The images in rock art, commonly seen along trails and at the locations mentioned in song itineraries, are *o'ohadag*. *O'ohadag* are also found on O'odham calendar sticks (*hikanaba*), which in many ways resemble musical rasps. The designs on rasps document spiritual song journeys in geographic space, whereas calendar sticks provide a temporal or chronological itinerary—a time line—relating the present to the past. This is an important distinction between O'odham systems of geographical and historical reckoning.

O'odham calendar sticks typically are longer, straighter pieces of wood than rasps, but they, too, are notched at regular intervals, each notch representing a year (fig. 16.6). The calendar stick keeper places painted figures or incised and painted symbols alongside the notches as reminders of the events that distinguished that year from every other. Each calendar stick is unique to the calendar stick keeper, but the stick itself is like a page out of the shared history of all O'odham. The keeper might pass the stick and its historical narrative on to a successor, or it might be buried with him at his funeral. The historical narrative and the symbols for each event become part of the stick itself, just as songs become part of scraping sticks. Even after the keeper has died, the stick remains a repository of personal historical knowledge.

We know the histories told by only a few of the calendar sticks that have survived, when their accounts were written down in English. These histories generally span the mid-nineteenth to the early twentieth century and mainly record events of central interest to the O'odham, including battles with Apaches, deaths, famines, epidemics, and ceremonies. As objects, calendar sticks provide rare insights into O'odham historical reckoning. The excerpt presented in the sidebar, covering the years from 1888 to 1891, offers a glimpse into the events people sought to remember.

Blackwater Calendar Stick Events

1888–89. A Papago [Tohono O'odham] who knew the Bluebird series of songs sang for the Santan people during the festival held by them. The captain of the native police and the calendrist went to Fort McDowell with three other men to act as scouts for the soldiers stationed there. During the year an epidemic carried away three prominent men at Blackwater.

1889–90. The wife of the head chief died.

1890–91. In the spring of 1891 occurred the last and most disastrous of the Gila floods. The Maricopa and Phoenix Railroad bridge was swept away, and the channels of both the Gila and Salt Rivers were changed in many places. The destruction of cultivated lands led to the change of the Salt River Pimas from the low bottoms to the mesas.

—Translated by Frank Russell, *The Pima Indians, 1908, 61–62*

Descriptions of calendar stick narration also suggest that O'odham recited their histories in much the same way they sang song cycles. Just as songs had to be sung in the correct geographical sequence, historical narratives had to be told in the correct chronological order. O'odham songs and historical reckonings are performed in similar ways, but songs describe space and histories describe time. This distinction certainly did not escape O'odham singers and calendar stick keepers.

Are the marks on calendar sticks similar to the song marks described for scraping sticks in the penultimate Oriole song? We think that this is likely. Historical recitations establish the present in reference to past events, in much the same way song journeys describe a spatial universe composed of interconnected spiritual places where things happen. Each provides the community with a path toward spatial and temporal awareness. Designs (*o'ohadag*) on rasps are abstract representations of songs, which describe spiritual events associated with particular places. Their counterparts on calendar sticks represent historical events.

Figure 16.8. A song flower (*ñe'ñei hiosig*) on a rasping stick. Song flowers may appear as designs representing flowers, mountains, or other figures or as the notched cross shown here (center).

Sacred Landscapes and History

What does all of this mean? We suggest that much of Native American infrastructure derives from traditional knowledge that relates ideas to facilities such as trails that allow societies to function. In the case of the O'odham, the retelling of song journeys generates a shared knowledge of O'odham geography, defined by significant places and the connections among them—by important sites and the spiritual events that happened there. Calendar stick histories explain the present in terms of past events. Known calendar stick histories begin in the nineteenth century, a time of substantial and sometimes catastrophic change in the O'odham world. Tribal histories describe in O'odham terms the cumulative effects of non-Indian incursions into their land and the disruption of their social relations and traditions.

How old are O'odham songscapes? Archaeological evidence reveals that the places the songs describe have been in use since the time of the Hohokam, centuries before Vincent Joseph's gift of the Oriole songs to anthropologists. Does the great age of these trails and sites mean that Hohokam people undertook spiritual as well as practical journeys similar to those of the O'odham? We do not know how the meanings of the paths and places may have changed for succeeding populations, but the fact that today's O'odham songscape trails connect these sacred sites of the past demonstrates their continued importance to the O'odham today.

Songscapes refer to the spatial and spiritual order of places and things, not to historical events. It is in this sense that they can be related to spiritual travels such as the salt pilgrimage. Through dreaming and song performance, O'odham singers raise their consciousness of the landscape.

What is the future of O'odham song? Modern development obscures traditional landscapes every day, yet songscapes continue to exist as new generations learn the songs from their elders. Without the songs, little would be left of the traditional O'odham worldview or of the sacred landscapes they portray. Working together, traditional community members and archaeologists may be able to recover ancient landscapes. O'odham trail archaeology, in particular, benefits enormously by taking into account the song journey described in the Oriole series. By learning about the traditional songscapes and the geographies they describe, archaeologists can hope to recover both the physical traces of past landscapes and their meanings for the people who created them. For the O'odham, their land persists in the songs and the songscapes they create. The final Oriole song, translated by Barnaby V. Lewis, says:

> The songs are ending as they go their
>   separate ways.
> From the center of our songs, the wind
>   comes,
> Flowing back and forth,
> Erasing the tracks of the people [preparing
>   the ground for future sings],
> Ready to place them here again.

J. Andrew Darling is program coordinator for the Cultural Resource Management Program of the Gila River Indian Community, Arizona. He is a cofounder of the Mexico-Norte Research Network. His research topics include ethnohistory, Native American witchcraft and religious institutions, and settlement patterns. Barnaby V. Lewis is a cultural resource specialist with the Gila River Indian Community, consulting with federal and state agencies and the archaeological community regarding repatriation and protection of human remains. He is an enrolled member of the Gila River Indian Community, Pima Tribe of southern Arizona, and is well known for cultural preservation efforts, particularly in keeping alive the songs of the Akimel O'odham.

This essay represents the views of its authors only. It does not in any way represent the views of the Gila River Indian Community, its members, or the O'odham of other communities in the United States or Mexico.

Figure 17.1. As in Hohokam times, a canal carries water past the Pueblo Grande platform mound (foreground) to supply a dense population in the Phoenix Basin.

The Hohokam
The Who and the Why

George J. Gumerman

In the winter of 1960, as a first-year graduate student on a field trip, I stood on an early version of a platform mound at the most famous of all Hohokam sites, Snaketown. My professor, Emil Haury, the man who largely defined Hohokam culture, intoned: "It is easy to see why one of the largest Hohokam sites was located where it was—the lush environment." I looked slack-jawed at the mostly barren landscape, the ground studded with a few clumps of grass and the occasional cactus, a couple of creosote bushes, and a lonely cottonwood tree (fig. 17.2). True, early Euro-Americans had dammed the Gila River upstream, so the area now looked bleaker than it had prehistorically. But I had grown up spending summer vacations in the north woods of Wisconsin, a place I considered truly lush. The woods and lakes teemed with deer, birds, berry bushes, rabbits, and fish. It took much of the next fifty years to gradually convince myself that the homeland of the Hohokam was indeed a bountiful desert, capable of supporting a large and technologically sophisticated society.

The Hohokam were supremely adapted to wresting a living out of what superficially appears to be a desolate environment. Changes in Hohokam society through time demonstrate that they developed an increasingly complex way of managing people and resources, and inhabitants of each environmental zone found slightly different ways of coping with local challenges. The major drainages of Hohokam territory contain rich soil that needs only the application of water to supply food for large numbers of people (plate 14). The uplands bordering the valleys harbored large and small game, supported edible wild plants, and provided raw materials such as turquoise, obsidian, and basalt for manos and metates.

At the time I stood on the Snaketown mound, Hohokam archaeology was in its infancy, lagging behind the rest of the Southwest. Snaketown was one of the few Hohokam sites yet excavated. It was as if an archaeologist in the future tried to understand present-day American society after excavating just Manhattan, without studying the country's Tucsons and Tallahassees. Why the late start for Hohokam archaeology? Unlike ruins in the Ancestral Pueblo country to the north, Hohokam remains visible on the surface lack the dramatic effect of cliff dwellings such as those at Mesa Verde or the stunning stone architecture of Chaco Canyon. Aside

Figure 17.2. Aerial view of the Snaketown area today.

Figure 17.3. Standing walls of even the largest Hohokam buildings are rarely visible. Before excavation, melted adobe from the upper walls and roof obscured the outline of even this compound with platform mounds at Casa Grande.

from the ruins of ball courts and platform mounds, the most one sees even on the largest Hohokam sites is low, unimpressive heaps of hearth and a scattering of potsherds (fig. 17.3). Moreover, Hohokam sites lie scattered over much of south-central Arizona, not manageably concentrated as at Mesa Verde or Chaco Canyon. Another reason was simply the climate. At the time I first visited Snaketown, almost all archaeology was done by university professors whose only available time for fieldwork was during the summer—unbearably hot in the Sonoran Desert.

After World War II, the pace of Hohokam archaeological research quickly caught up with and even surpassed that of work to the north. The growing use of air conditioning was one factor that touched off the population shift of Americans to the Arizona desert that continues to this day. The new-comers wanted to live where the majority of the Hohokam had lived, and for the same reason—the availability of surface water. The population explosion caused a great loss of Hohokam sites, which were paved over for parking lots or fell victim to other construction projects. With time, however, antiquities laws passed by federal, state, and even local governments required that archaeological sites be explored before they were destroyed. Ironically, increasing population and development then began to open up hundreds of sites to excavation and

helped create a small industry in archaeological research.

Archaeologists view the societies they study through the dimensions of space and time, attempting to understand how each society developed and changed and how its members arranged themselves on the landscape. The Hohokam started out as relatively simple village farmers with few apparent class distinctions in the first several centuries before the common era. Their major food crops of corn, beans, and squash (fig. 17.4) had come to them from what is now Mexico (oddly, unaccompanied by the chile pepper, which arrived with Spanish colonists centuries later). Also from Mexico came ideas and institutions that set Hohokam society on a trajectory that eventually included large populations, class distinctions, massive irrigation networks, public buildings in the form of ball courts and platform mounds, and elaborate, distinctive crafts.

The transition from a hunting and gathering life-style to settled village farming, great increases in population, and the emergence of hierarchical societies took place hundreds of times in world prehistory; it was not unique to the Hohokam. What is unique about the Hohokam is the details that distinguish them from other peoples who passed through the same stages. Like contemporary societies whose members are organized into units ranging from the family, the neighborhood, and the

Figure 17.4. Corn and other major Hohokam crops were first domesticated in Mexico.

In the courtyards, residents carried out their daily tasks, socialized, and rested. It is doubtful that the Hohokam in this mild climate actually did much "living" inside their houses, as we do. Normal household tasks were probably confined to the pithouses only during rare spells of inclement weather. Despite —or perhaps because of—the use of the courtyard as a common area, residents kept the ground clean of everyday artifacts and trash. "Waste management" was highly regarded: all large Hohokam sites have designated areas where trash was deposited so regularly that it became mounded. Often these "trash mounds" are spatially linked to individual courtyards.

The village, consisting of a number of courtyard groups, was part of a still larger network of people in Hohokam society. The remains of a village are what archaeologists commonly call a site. Presumably, the residents of the larger and more elaborate houses in the village were important in making villagewide decisions and held at least persuasive influence over their fellow villagers. All the villages along the canal lines supplied by a common intake on the river made up an irrigation community. Much the way a contemporary road map reveals the interconnectedness of modern cities, a map of a Hohokam irrigation system displays the interconnectedness of the villages along its canals. Even more than road systems today, irrigation networks indicate interdependence and cooperation among a clearly defined set of villages.

Irrigation networks, no matter where they occur in the world, signal to the archaeologist a high

local community to the nation state, the Hohokam arranged themselves into social units that varied in size and increased in number and complexity during the Hohokam millennium.

The smallest and most persistent social form was the household, as it is in all human societies. Houses were arranged around a common open space called a courtyard. The people living in the houses surrounding a courtyard made up an extended family that controlled designated crop land in the irrigated areas. Especially in large settlements in the Phoenix Basin, these courtyard groups had great longevity, sometimes as many as seven generations, implying something along the lines of what we would call "estate planning." Other families avoided encroaching on existing courtyard groups, sometimes for more than 150 years. Clearly, some form of social identity was associated with the courtyard. Although at first few status differences appear between households, by the ninth century CE we see distinctions between low-status and high-status households. The wealthier households were much larger, and their dwellings were of higher quality.

degree of planning and cooperation for construction and maintenance, as well as a social system that allows for the allocation of that scarce and essential resource, water. The Hohokam canal networks, therefore, imply an orderly system for coordination that involved all the villages they linked. Without formal rules for sharing and cooperation, the villages nearest the intake on the river could have hoarded all the water for themselves and their nearest neighbors when supplies were low, leaving villages with fields toward the end of the system dry. Yet despite the need for cooperation and sharing, we can infer that settlements making up an irrigation community were hierarchically arranged, because a few were much larger than the others and held the only buildings for public gatherings and rituals.

Archaeologists identify another kind of Hohokam community, one composed of a cluster of settlements that shared in communal rituals at public buildings in a large central village. The lengthier irrigation networks often included several such clusters. The ball court community, the set of settlements surrounding a center with a ball court, came into existence about 700 CE and became the predominant form of Hohokam settlement organization until 1050 or 1100, when people stopped building these public facilities. Ball courts are among the trademark Hohokam traits that owed their existence to inspiration from the high cultures of Mexico.

Like our own baseball stadiums, Hohokam ball courts had no standard format or dimensions but varied greatly in form and size. Presumably, they were constructed under the supervision of an elite group or headman. Perhaps again like our modern baseball, the Hohokam ball game was imbued with ritual and integrated a number of villages. The larger courts could accommodate as many as 700 spectators. Much the way saints' days in medieval European cathedral towns provided occasions for people to barter, gamble, meet prospective spouses, and gossip, so were ball court events opportunities for the Hohokam to interact. The ball court center represents its community's focal point for the ritual and social activity that was the glue holding Hohokam society together.

Ball courts extended outside Hohokam territory to the northwest into the Prescott area and north to the vicinity of Flagstaff, indicating that the Hohokam exerted some sort of ritual influence on other Southwestern groups. Interestingly, ball courts on the periphery of the Hohokam world lasted longer than those in the core area. This suggests that the courts of the Hohokam core were more intimately tied in to a coherent ritual system than were those in outlying regions, so their use ceased when the system collapsed.

The incursion of Hohokam people and cultural influence into the north and west was not a one-way street. Later in the Hohokam sequence, during the twelfth and thirteenth centuries, Ancestral Pueblo immigrants from the north settled in Classic period Hohokam territory. These centuries were times of upheaval and great population movements in the north, and presumably that is why northerners moved into the Hohokam area. Continuing for many decades, these migrations from north to south created a variety of new social relationships between migrants and long-time inhabitants.

The collapse of the ball court ritual system around 1100 and residents' departure from some of the previous ball court centers, including the important village of Snaketown, suggest that a reorganization of Hohokam society took place at that time. While the ball courts flourished, only a few sources of painted pottery existed in the Phoenix Basin, and potters at these Gila River locations supplied most of the red-on-buff ceramics for the entire Hohokam region. With the collapse of the ball court system, potters began to make painted wares locally, which suggests that the ball court events had provided the opportunities for barter that spread red-on-buff pottery so widely throughout the Hohokam world.

What caused the venerable and pervasive ball court system to collapse? Tree-ring data from the headwaters of the major streams that eventually flow into the Hohokam heartland show that the entire period of ball court community development and expansion was not only relatively wet but also consistently so, without great fluctuations in rainfall. The Hohokam world reached its greatest extent during this period. A consistent flow of life-supporting water would have been relatively easy to regulate and disperse to communities along the canals. Beginning in the twelfth century, less rain fell at times, and the amounts of water that could be allocated to settlements fluctuated widely. It is easy to imagine social strife arising when this precious commodity was in short supply or some irrigators got more of it than others. The weather pattern changed not only over what is now Arizona but also throughout much of the Southwest, and the same trend toward social disruption is seen in this larger region.

Although Hohokam society underwent a reorganization, the changes did not include a reduction in social hierarchy, for at about 1150 we see the beginnings of platform mound communities in the Hohokam core area. Indeed, Hohokam society was probably more hierarchically organized during the time of the platform mound communities than during the earlier ball court community era. Whether platform mounds were built as underpinnings primarily for ritual structures, elite residences, or both, they indicate broad community influence for the leaders who officiated over communal events in these precincts. It is a worldwide phenomenon that higher-status persons are accorded a physically higher plane than "ordinary" people—high status is indeed indicated by height. Whereas ball courts hint at ritual activity centered on "games," platform mounds and their enclosing walls imply that some persons were segregated by status from the rest of the society. As in the case of ball courts, the largest platform mounds and the greatest concentration of them are found in the Phoenix Basin. The distribution of platform mounds only partially corresponds to the earlier locations of ball courts, so platform mounds did not simply replace ball courts in existing centers and their surrounding communities (compare maps 3 and 4).

The basic Hohokam social units, from small courtyard groups to ball court and platform mound communities, are relatively easy to understand. But who were the Hohokam in their entirety, living as they did across 50,000 square miles in central and southern Arizona? Were they a single tribe or ethnic group bound by a common language? A political entity? Subscribers to a shared ideological

system? All of the above? The area where the Salt and Gila Rivers converge—the Phoenix Basin—was the densely populated core of Hohokam society, but even there, no evidence confirms the existence of an overarching political entity that encompassed distinct irrigation communities on separate canal networks. The southern Hohokam area, centered in Tucson, like areas on the northern periphery and boundary areas elsewhere, was less populous and reveals fewer apparent status differences than the Phoenix Basin.

Linking everyone in the Hohokam world was a distinctive iconography—designs found everywhere on pottery, shell ornaments, and carved stone, from artifacts in the simplest structures to those on platform mounds. Today, jewelry designers put Hohokam designs, especially the lively Preclassic images of birds, amphibians, and reptiles, on countless silver earrings, necklaces, and pins. Hohokam designs even grace the concrete overpasses of southern Arizona's interstate highways. The pervasiveness of these designs, along with the characteristic cremations of the dead during the Preclassic period—a practice found among few other cultural groups in the prehistoric Southwest—suggests that an ideological bond led the Hohokam to identify themselves as a distinct group. The designs were among the badges of membership that bound all Hohokam people together. It seems that political centralization at a large scale remained weak throughout the Hohokam millennium, whereas social and religious institutions integrated broad areas.

What happened to the Hohokam communities before the Spanish *entrada* into what is now southern Arizona in the late 1600s? The Spaniards wrote about scattered villages and mentioned large ruins such as Casa Grande, but they made no note of huge irrigation systems, ball courts, platform mounds, or elites. In southern Arizona, as in most of the Southwest, the complex societies that flourished in earlier eras were gone when the Spaniards arrived. The Chaco Canyons, Casas Grandes, Mesa Verdes, and Snaketowns were no more. We have an unfortunate tendency to view past societies as short-lived, as having failed to sustain themselves, but the Hohokam were a resilient people who thrived and adapted to change for more than a thousand years. Snaketown maintained its exemplary role as an important center for more than 500 years. It was only in 1976 that the United States celebrated its bicentennial—a fraction of the time the Hohokam existed as a recognized entity.

Although Spaniards encountered only village farmers in seventeenth-century southern Arizona, the historical continuity between their descendants in the region today, the O'odham, and the more complexly organized Hohokam cannot be denied. This continuity was brought home to me dramatically in a "repatriation" ceremony in 2001. Until May of that year, the artifacts and cremation burials from excavations at Snaketown in the 1930s and 1960s had been housed at the Arizona State Museum, on the campus of the University of Arizona. As the director of the museum at the time, I was honored to be involved in seeing these items returned to the Akimel O'odham for reburial (fig. 17.5). The governor and elders of the Gila River Indian Community tearfully chanted the "Going Home" song while the remains and artifacts were loaded into a truck for the trip back to the Community.

Figure 17.5. George Gumerman, then director of the Arizona State Museum, and Donald Antone, governor of the Gila River Indian Community, finalize the repatriation of Snaketown artifact collections in 2001.

Anybody witnessing this moving event would have been convinced of the connection between the prehistoric Hohokam and the contemporary O'odham.

George J. Gumerman is a senior scholar at the School for Advanced Research in Santa Fe, New Mexico, and previously served as its interim president and as vice president for academic affairs at the Santa Fe Institute. From 1997 to 2002 he was director of the Arizona State Museum at the University of Arizona, Tucson. He edited the milestone book *Exploring the Hohokam: Desert Peoples of the American Southwest* (1991).

Suggested Reading

The magazines *American Archaeology*, published by the Archaeological Conservancy, and *Archaeology Southwest*, published by the Center for Desert Archaeology, frequently include brief accounts of important new findings in Sonoran Desert archaeology. Other books and articles we recommend are as follows.

Abbott, David R.
2000   *Ceramics and Community Organization among the Hohokam*. University of Arizona Press, Tucson.

Bahr, Donald, Lloyd Paul, and Vincent Joseph
1997   *Ants and Orioles: Showing the Art of Pima Poetry*. University of Utah Press, Salt Lake City.

Bahr, Donald, Juan Smith, William Allison, and Julian Hayden
1994   *The Hohokam Chronicles: The Short Swift Time of Gods on Earth*. University of California Press, Berkeley.

Bayman, James M.
2001   "The Hohokam of Southwest North America." *Journal of World Prehistory*, vol. 15, no. 3, pp. 257–311.
2002   "Hohokam Craft Economies and the Materialization of Power." *Journal of Archaeological Method and Theory*, vol. 9, no. 1, pp. 69–95.

Bostwick, Todd W.
2002   *Landscape of the Spirits: Hohokam Rock Art at South Mountain Park*. University of Arizona Press, Tucson.

Clark, Jeffery J.
2001   *Tracking Prehistoric Migrations: Pueblo Settlers among the Tonto Basin Hohokam*. Anthropological Papers of the University of Arizona, no. 65. University of Arizona Press, Tucson.

Cobb, Charles R., Jeffery Maymon, and Randall H. McGuire
1997   "Feathered, Horned, and Antlered Serpents: Mesoamerican Connections with the Southwest and Southeast." In *Great Towns and Regional Polities in the Prehistoric American Southwest and Southeast*, edited by Jill E. Neitzel, pp. 165–181. University of New Mexico Press, Albuquerque.

Craig, Douglas B.
1998   "Labor Investment and Organization in Platform Mound Construction: A Case from the Tonto Basin of Central Arizona." *Journal of Field Archaeology*, vol. 25, no. 3, pp. 245–59.

Crown, Patricia L.
1994   *Ceramics and Ideology: Salado Polychrome Pottery*. University of New Mexico Press, Albuquerque.

Crown, Patricia L., and W. James Judge (editors)
1991   *Chaco and Hohokam: Prehistoric Regional Systems in the American Southwest*. SAR Press, Santa Fe.

Darling, J. Andrew, John C. Ravesloot, and Michael Waters
2004   "Village Drift and Riverine Settlement: Modeling Akimel O'Odham Land Use." *American Anthropologist*, vol. 106, no. 2, pp. 282–95.

Doyel, David E., Suzanne K. Fish, and Paul R. Fish
2000   *The Hohokam Village Revisited.* American
        Association for the Advancement of Science,
        Southwestern and Rocky Mountain Division,
        Fort Collins, Colorado.

Elson, Mark D.
1998   *Expanding the View of Hohokam Platform Mounds:
        An Ethnographic Perspective.* Anthropological
        Papers of the University of Arizona, no. 63.
        University of Arizona Press, Tucson.

Fish, Paul R., and Suzanne K. Fish
1994   "Southwest and Northwest: Recent Research at
        the Juncture of the United States and Mexico."
        Journal of Archaeological Research, vol. 2, no. 1,
        pp. 3–44.

Fish, Suzanne K.
2000   "Hohokam Impacts on Sonoran Desert
        Environment." In *Imperfect Balance: Landscape
        Transformations in the Precolumbian Americas,*
        edited by David Lentz, pp. 251–80. Columbia
        University Press, New York.

Fish, Suzanne K., Paul R. Fish, and John H. Madsen
1992   *The Marana Community in the Hohokam World.*
        Anthropological Papers of the University of
        Arizona, no. 56. University of Arizona Press,
        Tucson.

Gumerman, George J. (editor)
1991   *Exploring the Hohokam: Prehistoric Desert
        Farmers of the American Southwest.* University of
        New Mexico Press, Albuquerque.

Haury, Emil W.
1976   *The Hohokam: Desert Farmers and Craftsmen.*
        University of Arizona Press, Tucson.

Hill, J. Brett, Jeffery J. Clark, William H. Doelle, and
Patrick D. Lyons
2005   "Prehistoric Demography in the Southwest:
        Migration, Coalescence, and Hohokam
        Population Decline." *American Antiquity,* vol. 69,
        no. 4, pp. 689–716.

Hunt, Robert C., David Guillet, David R. Abbott,
James Bayman, Paul Fish, Suzanne Fish, Keith Kintigh,
and James A. Neely
2005   "Plausible Ethnographic Analogies for the Social
        Organization of Hohokam Canal Irrigation."
        American Antiquity, vol. 70, no. 3, pp. 433–56.

Mabry, Jonathan B.
2005   "Changing Knowledge and Ideas about the First
        Farmers in Southeastern Arizona." In *The Late
        Archaic across the Borderlands: From Foraging to
        Farming,* edited by Bradley J. Vierra, pp. 41–83.
        University of Texas Press, Austin.

Phillips, Steven J., and Patricia W. Comus
2000   *A Natural History of the Sonoran Desert.* Arizona-
        Sonora Desert Museum, Tucson, and University
        of California Press, Berkeley.

Ravesloot, John C., and Michael R. Waters
2003   "Geoarchaeology and Archaeological Site
        Patterning on the Middle Gila River, Arizona."
        Journal of Field Archaeology, vol. 29, nos. 1–2,
        pp. 203–14.

Rea, Amadeo
1997   *At the Desert's Green Edge: An Ethnobotany of the
        Gila River Pima.* University of Arizona Press,
        Tucson.

Russell, Frank
1908   *The Pima Indians.* 26th Annual Report of the
        Bureau of American Ethnology for the Years
        1904-1905. GPO: Washington, DC.

Underhill, Ruth
1939   *Social Organization of the Papago Indians.*
        Columbia University Press, New York.

Wallace, Henry D.
2003   *Roots of Sedentism: Archaeological Excavations at
        Valencia Vieja, a Founding Village in the Tucson
        Basin of Southern Arizona.* Anthropological Papers,
        no. 29, Center for Desert Archaeology, Tucson.

Wells, E. C., Glen Rice, and John C. Ravesloot
2004   "Peopling Landscapes between Villages in the
        Middle Gila River Valley of Central Arizona."
        American Antiquity, vol. 69, no. 4, pp. 627–52.

Whittlesey, Stephanie M., R. Ciolek-Torello, and
J. H. Altschul (editors)
1997   *Vanishing River: Landscapes and Lives of the Lower
        Verde Valley.* SRI Press, Tucson.

Wilcox, David R.
1991   "The Mesoamerican Ballgame in the American
        Southwest." In *The Mesoamerican Ballgame,* edit-
        ed by Vernon Scarborough and David R. Wilcox,
        pp. 101–25. University of Arizona Press, Tucson.

Picture Credits

Color section, after page 34: Plates 1–4, photographs by Helga Teiwes, courtesy ASM; plate 5, photograph by Ken Matesich, courtesy ASM; plate 7, drawing by Pamela Key; plate 8, photograph by Paul Fish; plate 9, painting by Michael Hampshire for Pueblo Grande Museum, City of Phoenix; plate 10, photograph by Helga Teiwes, courtesy ASM; plate 11, courtesy Los Angeles County Museum of Art; plates 12 and 13, photographs by Adriel Heisey; plate 14, photograph by Helga Teiwes, courtesy ASM; plate 15, photograph by Adriel Heisey; plate 16, photograph by Helga Teiwes, courtesy ASM; plate 17 photograph by Adriel Heisey, courtesy Henry Wallace; courtesy ASM; plate 15, plates 16 and 17, photographs by Helga Teiwes, courtesy ASM; plate 18, © SAR, drawn by Molly O'Halloran; plate 19, photograph by Paul Fish; plate 20, photograph by Helga Teiwes, courtesy ASM; plate 21, map by Douglas Craig, adapted by Matthew Hill; plate 22, watercolor by Arthur Schott, courtesy ASM; plate 23, photograph by Walter McQuarry, courtesy ASM.

Front matter: Frontispiece (ii–iii): detail of photograph by Helga Teiwes, courtesy ASM; maps 1–4 (vii–x): © 2007 SAR, drawn by Molly O'Halloran; dedication (xii): photograph by Helga Teiwes, courtesy ASM.

Chapter One: Fig. 1.1, photograph by Helga Teiwes, courtesy ASM; fig. 1.2, plate 43 in J. W. Fewkes, Casa Grande, Arizona, 28th Annual Report of the BAE, 1906–1907 (Washington, D.C.: GPO, 1912); fig. 1.3, map facing p. 12 in Omar Turney, Prehistoric Irrigation in Arizona (Phoenix: Arizona State Historian, 1929); fig. 1.4, courtesy ASM; fig.1.5, photograph by Helga Teiwes, courtesy ASM; fig. 1.6, photograph by Matts Myhrman; fig. 1.7, photograph by Charles Miksicek, courtesy Suzanne K. Fish; fig. 1.8, photograph by Helga Teiwes, courtesy ASM.

Chapter Two: Figs. 2.1 and 2.2, photographs by Henry Wallace; fig. 2.3, photograph by Adriel Heisey in Henry Wallace (ed.), Roots of Sedentism (Tucson: Center for Desert Archaeology, 2003); fig. 2.4, adapted from fig. 14.8 in Henry Wallace (ed.) Roots of Sedentism; fig. 2.5, photograph by Henry Wallace; fig. 2.6, adapted from fig. 15.5 in Henry Wallace (ed.), Roots of Sedentism; fig. 2.7, photograph by Helga Teiwes, courtesy ASM.

Chapter Three: Fig. 3.1, photograph by Helga Teiwes, courtesy ASM; fig. 3.2, photograph by E.B. Sayles, courtesy ASM; figs. 3.3 and 3.4, photographs by Marianne Tyndall, courtesy Patricia Crown; fig. 3.5, photograph by William Dinwiddie, McGee Expedition 1894–1895, courtesy of Special Collections, University of Arizona Library; fig. 3.6, fig. 28 in F. Russell, The Pima Indians, 26th Annual Report of the BAE, 1904–1905 (Washington, D.C.: GPO, 1906); fig. 3.7, adapted from fig. 13.15 in Emil Haury, The Hohokam (Tucson: University of Arizona Press, 1976); fig. 3.8, courtesy LACMNH.

Chapter Four: Fig. 4.1, photograph by the Arizona Department of Transportation, courtesy Douglas Craig; fig. 4.2, map by Matthew Hill; fig. 4.3, photograph by William Dinwiddie, McGee Expedition 1894–1895, NMNH; fig. 4.4, fig. 5.43 in T. Kathleen Henderson, Hohokam Farming on the Salt River Floodplain (Tucson: Center for Desert Archaeology, 2003); fig. 4.5, photograph by Helga Teiwes, courtesy ASM.

Chapter Five: Fig. 5.1, courtesy David Doyel; fig. 5.2, photograph by Helga Teiwes, courtesy ASM; fig. 5.3, plate facing p. 92 in C. Lumholtz, New Trails in Mexico (New York: Charles Scribner's Sons, 1912); figs. 5.4 and 5.5, adapted from figs. 3.8 and 3.2 in S. Fish et al., "Evolution and structure of the Classic period Marana Community," The Marana Community in the Hohokam World, edited by S. Fish, P. Fish, and J. Madsen (Tucson: University of Arizona Press, 1992); fig. 5.6, adapted from 13.2 in S. Fish, "Dynamics of scale," Interpreting Southwestern Diversity: Underlying Principles and Overarching Patterns, edited by P. Fish and J. Reid (Tempe: Department of Anthropology, Arizona State University, 1996); fig 5.7, adapted from fig. 2 in Patricia Crown, "Classic period Hohokam settlement and land use in the Casa Grande Ruin area, Arizona," Journal of Field Archaeology 14: 147–162; fig. 5.8, adapted from fig. 13.3 in S. Fish, "Dynamics of scale," Interpreting Southwestern Diversity: Underlying Principles and Overarching Patterns, edited by P. Fish and J. Reid (Tempe: Department of Anthropology, Arizona State University, 1996).

Chapter Six: Fig. 6.1, drawing by John Joha in collaboration with David Doyel, courtesy David Doyel; fig. 6.2, photograph by Thomas Lincoln, courtesy Bureau of Reclamation; fig. 6.3, courtesy ASM; fig. 6.4, frontispiece in David Jacobs, A Salado Platform Mound on Tonto Creek (Tempe: Department of Anthropology, Arizona State University, 1997), courtesy Charles Redman; fig. 6.5, adapted from fig.1 in J.W. Fewkes, Casa Grande, Arizona, 28th Annual Report of the BAE, 1906–1907 (Washington, D.C.: GPO, 1912); fig. 6.6, drawing by Ziba Ghassemi, fig. 1.10 in M. Elson, M. Stark, and D. Gregory, The Roosevelt Community Development Study: New Perspectives on Tonto Basin Prehistory (Tucson: Center for Desert Archaeology, 1995), courtesy Mark Elson; fig. 6.7, photograph by Helga Teiwes, courtesy ASM.

Chapter Seven: Fig. 7.1, fig. 12.84 in Emil Haury, The Hohokam (Tucson: University of Arizona Press, 1976), courtesy University of Arizona Press; fig. 7.2, photograph by Helga Teiwes, courtesy ASM; fig. 7.3, map by Matthew Hill; fig. 7.4, adapted from fig. 29 in Beatriz Braniff, "La tradición Chupícuro-Tolteca," La Gran Chichimeca, edited by Beatriz Braniff (Milan: Jaca Book); figs. 7.5 and 7.6, courtesy LACMNH; fig. 7.7, photograph by César Villalobos, courtesy Elisa Villalpando C.

Chapter Eight: Fig. 8.1, courtesy ASM; figs. 8.2, 8.3, and 8.4, plate 17 a, c, and d in F. Russell, The Pima Indians, 26th Annual Report of the BAE, 1904–1905 (Washington, D.C.: GPO, 1906); fig. 8.5, fig. 52 in F. Russell, The Pima Indians, 26th Annual Report of the BAE, 1904-1905; figs. 8.6 and 8.7, photographs by Helga Teiwes, courtesy ASM; fig. 8.8, photograph by Emil Haury, courtesy ASM.

Chapter Nine: Figs. 9.1, 9.2, and 9.3, photographs by Helga Teiwes, courtesy ASM; fig. 9.4, photograph by Helga Teiwes, fig. 7 in James Bayman, "Shell ornament consumption in a Classic Hohokam platform mound community center," Journal of Field Archaeology 23: 403–420 (1996), courtesy James Bayman; fig 9.5, photograph by Bruce D. Lindsay, courtesy ASM; fig. 9.6, photograph by Helga Teiwes, courtesy ASM.

Chapter Ten: Fig. 10.1, drawing by John Joha in collaboration with David Doyel, courtesy David Doyel; fig. 10.2, map by David Doyel; fig. 10.3, photograph by William Dinwiddie, McGee Expedition 1894-1895, NMNH; fig. 10.4, photograph by Helga Teiwes, courtesy ASM; fig. 10.5, drawing by Ben Mixon, courtesy David Doyel; fig. 10.6, courtesy David Doyel; fig. 10.7, adapted from maps by David Gregory and Emil Haury, courtesy David Doyel.

Chapter Eleven: Fig. 11.1, photograph by Ruth Greenspan; figs. 11.2 and 11.3, maps © SAR, drawn by Molly O'Halloran; fig. 11.4, courtesy ASM; fig. 11.5, map by Matthew Hill; fig. 11.6, photograph by Homer Shantz, courtesy Shantz Archive, University of Arizona Herbarium; fig. 11.7, photograph by Helga Teiwes, courtesy ASM.

Chapter Twelve: Fig 12.1, fig. 1.2 in Jeffrey Clark and Patrick Lyons (eds.), *Migrants and Mounds: Classic Period Archaeology in the Lower San Pedro Valley* (Tucson: Center for Desert Archaeology, 2007), courtesy Jeffrey Clark; fig. 12.2, photograph by Richard W. Lord, courtesy ASM; fig. 12.3, front cover of Jeffrey Clark, *Tracking Prehistoric Migrations: Pueblo Settlers among the Tonto Basin Hohokam* (Tucson: University of Arizona Press, 2001), courtesy Jeffrey Clark; fig. 12.4, fig. 6.7 in Jeffrey Clark and Patrick Lyons (eds.), *Migrants and Mounds: Classic Period Archaeology in the Lower San Pedro Valley* (Tucson: Center for Desert Archaeology, 2007), courtesy Jeffrey Clark; fig. 12.5, adapted from Alexander J. Lindsay, Jr., Richard Ambler, Mary Anne Stein, and Philip M. Hobler, *Survey and Excavations North and East of Navajo Mountain, Utah* (Flagstaff: Museum of Northern Arizona, 1968); fig. 12.6, photograph by Peter J. Pilles, courtesy Sharlot Hall Museum; fig. 12.7, photograph by Patrick D. Lyons; fig. 12.8, plate 5, in Charles Di Peso, *The Reeve Ruin of Southeastern Arizona* (Dragoon, Arizona: Amerind Foundation, 1958) courtesy John Ware.

Chapter Thirteen: Fig. 13.1, photograph by Adriel Heisey; fig. 13.2, photograph by D. F. Mitchell, courtesy Palace of the Governors, Museum of New Mexico; fig. 13.3, photograph by Paul Fish; figs. 13.4, 13.5, and 13.6, courtesy ASM; fig. 13.7, photograph by Paul Fish.

Chapter Fourteen: Fig. 14.1, courtesy ASM; fig. 14.2, photograph by Paul Fish; fig. 14.3, plate 19d in Frank Russell, *The Pima Indians*, 26th Annual Report of the BAE, 1904-1905 (Washington, D.C.: GPO, 1906); fig. 14.4,

courtesy ASM; fig. 14.5, plate CXIV in Cosmos Mindeleff, *The Repair of the Casa Grande Ruin*, 15th Annual Report of the BAE 1893-94 (Washinton, D.C.: GPO, 1897).

Chapter Fifteen: Fig. 15.1, watercolor by Arthur Schott, courtesy ASM; fig. 15.2, print facing p. 87 in W.H. Emory, *Notes of a Military Reconnaissance, from Fort Leavenworth in Missouri to San Diego, California* (Washington, D.C.: Wendell and Van Benthuysen, 1848); figs. 15.3 and 15.4, courtesy Arizona Historical Society; fig. 15.5, photograph by Edward S. Curtis, courtesy ASM.

Chapter Sixteen: Fig. 16.1, photograph by Andrew Darling; fig. 16.2, map by Lynn Simon, courtesy Cultural Resources Program, Gila River Indian Community; fig. 16.3, photograph by Barnaby Lewis; fig. 16.4, map by Lynn Simon, drawn from Donald Bahr, Lloyd Paul, and Vincent Joseph, *Ants and Orioles: Showing the Art of Pima Poetry* (Salt Lake City: University of Arizona, 1997); fig. 16.5, photograph by Andrew Darling; fig. 16.6, photograph by Edward H. Davis, courtesy NMAI; fig. 16.7, photograph of rasping sticks by Melissa Altamirano, photograph of calendar sticks by Josh Roffler, both courtesy Cultural Resources Program, Gila River Indian Community, and inset photograph by Edward H. Davis, courtesy NMAI.

Chapter Seventeen: Fig. 17.1, photograph by Adriel Heisey; fig. 17.2, photograph by Emil Haury, courtesy ASM; fig. 17.3, plate 28 in J. W. Fewkes, *Casa Grande, Arizona*, 28th Annual Report of the BAE, 1906–1907 (Washington, D.C.: GPO, 1912); fig. 17.4, photograph by Helga Teiwes, courtesy ASM; fig. 17.5, photograph by Geoffrey Ashley, courtesy ASM.

Index

Metates, 85

Micaceous schist, 67, *71*, 84

Middle Gila Buff Ware, 101, 102, 104

Migrations: of Ancestral Puebloans, *99*, 99–100, **100**, 103–105, *104*, *105*, *106*; Classic period, 144; of Hohokam from Mesoamerica, 59, 65; of Hohokam from West Mexico, 13, 14; of O'odham, 131–136; into Tonto Basin, 5

Mindeleff, Cosmos, 110

Mindeleff, Victor, 110

Mirrors, 61, *61*

Mogollon influence, 101

Mother-daughter communities, 41

Motifs: bird eating snake, *28*, 59, *60*, *70*; frogs/toads, 71, 81; Mesoamerican influence, 59–60, *60*; pervasiveness, 145; Preclassic, *64*; of trade, *86*; and water, 69, 71–72

Motz, Fisher, *111*

Mountains, beliefs about, 69–70, 71–72, 133

Music, *48*, 131–139, *138*, 146

Mythology, *56*, 119, 125–129

Name derivation, 115

National Environmental Policy Act (1970), 112

National Historic Preservation Act (1966), 112

Nelson, Ben, 58

Nials, Fred, 96

Northern Tucson Basin Project, 113–114

Obsidian, 78, 104

Older persons, role of, 28

O'odham: craft traditions, 75; history records, 125–129, 137–139; language, 5, 123; music, 131–139, *138*; pottery firing, *68*; sacred sites, 119–120; trade, 84, *85*, 123; traditions about collapse, 9; traditions about Hohkam, 115, 117–121, 125–129; view of excavations, 120–121; Vikita ceremony, 42. *See also* Akimel O'odham; Tohono O'odham

O'ohadag, 136–137

Oral traditions, *56*, 119, 125–129, 137–139

Organ pipe cactus fruit, P22

Oriole song series, 133–135, **134**, 136, 139

Palettes: first appearance, 9; Preclassic period stone, *6*; raw material for, 67

Papago Freeway Project, 114

Papaguería, 77–78, 79

Pastes (pottery), 66–67

Patio groups, 60

Peasant farmer communities, 37

Phoenix, AZ, 1

Phoenix Basin: chiefdoms, 86; influence in northern San Pedro Valley, 101, 102; irrigation systems, 83, **83**, P20

Pima. *See* Akimel O'odham

Pima-Maricopa Irrigation Project, 93

Piman languages, 5

Pinkley, Nancy, *111*

Pioneer period: ball courts, 51; canals, 95; Mesoamerican influence, 59; social organization, 8–9; Valencia Vieja during, 17

Pithouses: aerial view, *14*, *108*; Grewe site, *30*, P21; in northern San Pedro Valley, 101–102; occupancy stability, *36*; Preclassic period, 13; reconstructed, P8; Valencia Vieja site, *16*

Place of the Snakes (Skoaquick), 91

Plain ware pottery, 66–67, 71, 102

Plant life. *See* Vegetation

Platform mounds, 52–54; Casa Grande National Monument, *142*, P17; Classic period, **x**; Cline Terrace site, *49*, *49*, *53*; distribution, 5, 40; in Gila River valley, **94**; importance, 4; labor requirements for building, 49, 54; Marana Mound site, P7; Mesa Grande, P12; in northern San Pedro Valley, 104; Preclassic period, 9; Pueblo Grande, 53, 54, *82*, *140*, P9; and social organization, 41, 145

Plazas, central, *6*, 18, *19*, 86

Political organization. *See* Leadership

Population: Classic period, 46, 88; growth, 19–20; labor requirements for building ball courts, 54; labor requirements for building canal systems, 5; labor requirements for building platform mounds, 49; labor requirements for building residences, 34–35; labor requirements for building ritual architecture, 54; lifespan, 29; in northern San Pedro Valley, 102, 105, 106; Preclassic period, 22; pre-Hohokam era, 13–15

Pottery: Classic period, 89; and collapse of ball court communities, 144; corrugated, **102**, 103; and diet, 19, 68; Early Ceramic period, 15; and geography, 65; instruction, 24–26, *25*; Maverick Mountain Polychrome, *99*, 104; Mesoamerican influence, 59, *60*; Middle Gila Buff Ware, 101, 102, 104; Mogollon influence, 101; pan-southwestern, 9; plain ware, 66–67, 71, 102; Preclassic period, *40*, *56*, *64*, 66–72, *69*, P5; producers, 23, 65–66; production, *26*, *66*, *67*, *67*, 67–68, *68*, 72, 103, *105*; raw materials, 66–67, 71, 71–72, 82, 104; red-on-brown, 101, 104, *105*; red-on-buff, 9, 19, 65,

84, 144, P5; religious significance, 68–69, 71, 72; Salado Polychrome, 63, 104, P6; trade, 79, 84, 85, *85*, 144; uses, 19, 68; vessel types, 68–69, *69*

Power Way, 89

Preclassic period: arrow points, 78–79, *80*, 81; ball courts, **ix**, 51; burials, 29; censers, *xiv*; hallmarks, 9; in northern San Pedro Valley, 101–102, *106*; palettes, *6*; platform mounds, 52; population, 22; pottery, *40*, *56*, *64*, 66–72, *69*, P5; residences, 13; rituals, *40*; shell ornaments, 77–78; stone vessels, 76, 76–77; territory, 9; trade, *57*

Pregnancy, 28

Prickly pear cactus, 7

Public buildings. *See* Ball courts; Platform mounds

Pueblo Grande platform mounds, 53, 54, *82*, *140*, P9

Qua-tha (Yavapai scout), *124*

Quetzalcoatl, 70

Raab, Mark, 113

Rainbow Way cult, 87

Rasping sticks, 136, *136*, *137*, *138*

Reddington site ball court, P13

Redman, Charles, 96

Red-on-brown pottery, 101, 104, *105*

Red-on-buff pottery: first appearance, 9; as Hohokam identifier, 65; popularity of, 19; Preclassic period, P5; as symbol of expansionist society, 84; trade, 144

Reed, Erik, 57, 59, *111*

Reeve Ruin, 103, 104

Religion: and agriculture, 72; ancestor worship, 18–19, *20*, 68; I'itoi, 119; Mesoamerican influence, *6*, *56*, 69–71, 72; and pottery, 68–69, 71, 72; sacred landscapes, 72; salt pilgrimages, 135; and water, 69–72. *See also* Ritual architecture; Rituals

Residences: after deaths, 29; compounds during Classic period, 88; cross-cultural comparisons of, 34; Early Ceramic period, 15; Kayenta immigrants, 103, *104*; of leadership, 17, *19*, 45; in Marana Community, 42, P7, P15; orientation, 15, 17; on platform mounds, 53; Preclassic period, 101–102, *106*; pre-pithouses, 14. *See also* Pithouses

Ritual architecture: defined, 50; importance of, 54–55; labor requirements for building, 49; Mesoamerican influence, 6; and social organization, 52, 53–54. *See also* Ball courts; Platform mounds

Rituals, *48*, 49–50; control and performance, 35, 39–40; Hohokam influence on Southwest, 144; and music, *48*, 131–139, *138*, 146; O'odham, *42*, 138–139; and palettes, *6*, *9*, *67*; and pottery, 68–69; Preclassic period, *40*; puberty ceremonies, 26; and sacred landscapes, 72, 118–120. *See also* Burials; Cremation

River People. *See* Akimel O'odham

Rock art, 137

Sacred landscapes, 72, 118–120, 138–139

Saguaro, *7*, P23

Salado culture, 59

Salado Polychrome, 63, 104, P6

Salt-Gila Aqueduct Project, 113, 114

Salt pilgrimages, 135

Salt River: Classic period communities, 45–46, **46**; irrigation systems, 83, **83**; platform mounds, 52, 54; watershed, 8

Salvage archaeology, 111–112

San Manuel district, 101, 103, 104

San Pedro Valley (northern): aerial view, P19; archaeological studies, 98, 100; migrations to, 100; Phoenix Basin influence, 101, 102; platform mounds, 104; population, 102, 105, 106; Preclassic period residences, 101–102, *106*

Sayles, E. B., *111*

Scraping sticks, 136, *136*

Sedentary period: canals, 95; effigy pots, P3, P4; Mesoamerican influence, 59; shell ornaments, P1

Serpents/snakes: in Mesoamerican religion, 70; in motifs, *28*, 59, *60*, *70*

Shackley, Steven, 78

Shell ornaments: bracelets, *74*, 81; manufacture, 77; rare, 81; Sedentary period, P1; sources of shells, 77–78; trade, 135; uses, 77; West Mexican influence, 61, 62–63, *63*

Sheridan, Thomas, 37

Sides (Akimel O'odham musician), *137*

Sings, 132–135

Sky Harbor project, 33, *34*

Snakes/serpents: in Mesoamerican religion, 70; in motifs, *28*, 59, *60*, *70*

Snaketown: abandoned, 94; aerial view, *90*, *141*; arrow points, 78–79, *80*, 81; ball court, *4*, *51*, *55*; Classic period, 88; courtyard groups, 31; excavations, 9–10, *111*, 112, *112*; importance of,

71, 72; irrigation, P18; name origination, 91; occupancy stability, 146; platform mounds, 52; political centralization, 87; as pottery production center, 72, 85; residences' orientation, 15, 17

Soalikee, Henry, *136*

Social identity, 39, 145

Social organization, 5–6; changes between Preclassic and Classic periods, 95–96; disappearance of coherent Hohkam, 9; evolution, 142–143, 144–145; kin-group based, 17, 18; Mesoamerican influence on, 142; Pioneer period, 8–9; of platform mound communities, 41, 145; and ritual architecture, 52, 53–54; and rituals, 35; units, 143–144. *See also* Courtyard groups; Leadership

Social singing, 132–135

Song flowers, 136, *138*

Songscapes, O'odham, 131–135, 138–139

Sonoran Desert: environment, *7*, *7–9*, *8*; traditions, 62–63

Southwest-Northwest peoples, 57

Spaniards, 9, 145–146

Stone, Lyle, 114

Stone implements: arrow points, *78*, 78–79; for food processing, 19, 27, *27*, 85; tools, *75*, 75–76

Stone vessels, *76*, 76–77

Stools, 78

Symbols: of leadership, 77, 79, 86, P2; of water, 69–70, 71–72

Temperatures, 8

Territory: boundaries of cultural hallmarks, 5; Preclassic period, 9; traditional tribal, **viii**

Thompson, Raymond, 114

Tlaloc cult, 69–71

Toad/frog motifs, 71, 81

Tohono O'odham: community relationships, 41; households, *32*; location, 125; pottery, *85*; pottery production, *26*; rituals, *42*; sacred sites, 118–120; saguaro camp, *116*; trade, 84, 85; traditional areas, **viii**; women, P22, P23

Tonto Basin culture, 5

Tools, *75*, 75–76

Tortolita phase, Tucson basin, **19**

Trade: and collapse of ball court communities, 144; in crafts, 79; extent, 84, 86;

jewelry, 135; Mesoamerican connection, 86; as motif, *86*; O'odham, 84, *85*, *123*; pottery, 79, 84, 85, *85*, 144; production of items for, 35; routes, **87**, 135; West Mexican connection, *6*, *57*, 61

Trails, 131–132, **132**, 133–136

Trincheras tradition, 62–63

Tucson basin communities: pithouses, *108*; Tortolita phase, **19**

Turney, Omar, 2

Turquoise mosaics, P2

Underhill, Ruth, 41, 84

Valencia Vieja site, 15; layout, 17, *18*; pithouses, *16*

Vegetation: cultivated, 8, 13–14, 42, *143*; Sonoran Desert, *7*, *7*, *8*, P22, P23; storage, 68

Ventana Cave, 119, *119*

Vikita ceremony, *42*

Wasley, William, 112

Waste management, 143

Water: and ball court communities, 144–145; and environmental changes, 88; irrigation systems, 1, 4, 5, 8, 83, **83**, **92**, *97*, 115; management, 37, 46, 84, 144; rainfall seasons, 7; in religion, 69–72; as source of conflict, 17; symbols of, 69–70, 71–72. *See also* Canal systems

Waters, Michael, 95, 96

Wealth, 34–35, 53–54

West Mexican culture: area, 58–59; Hohokam migrations, 13, 14; influence, 52, 61–63; and Mesoamerican culture, 63; trade, *6*, *57*, 61

Wilcox, David, 15, 31, 51, 81

Witch Telling, 125–129

Women: body adornment, 28; clothing, 27; hairstyles, *28*; occupations, 23, 26; O'odham, *122*, P22, P23

Woodbury, Richard, 36

Yavapais: language, 5, *123*; oral traditions, 126, 127, 128–129; scouts, *124*; traditional areas, **viii**

Yuman languages, 5

Zig-Zag Mountain, *130*, 131